CRAZY WISDOM
Tools for Evolving Consciousness

Tom Thresher

Published by Integral Publishers
http://www.integralpublishers.com
4845 E. 2nd St.
Tucson, AZ 85711
831 333-9200

Religion 2. Christianity 3. Philosophy

ISBN: 978-0-9904419-6-0

Cover design: QT Punque
Our printer certifies the following:
· All wood product components used in black & white, standard color, or select color paperback books, utilizing either cream or white bookblock paper, that are manufactured in the LaVergne, Tennessee Production Center are Sustainable Forestry Initiative® (SFI®) Certified Sourcing.
· All wood product components used in black & white, standard color, or select color paperback books, utilizing either cream or white bookblock paper that are manufactured the Allentown, Pennsylvania Production center are Sustainable Forestry Initiative® (SFI®) Certified Sourcing.
· The cream or white bookblock paper in black & white, standard color, or select color hardcover books manufactured in the LaVergne, Tennessee Production Center or the Allentown, Pennsylvania Production Center is Sustainable Forestry Initiative® (SFI®) Certified Sourcing.
· All wood product components used in black & white or standard color paperback books, utilizing either cream or white bookblock paper, or premium color paperbacks on white bookblock paper, that are manufactured in the Milton Keynes UK Production Center are Forest Stewardship Council® (FSC®) Mix Credit. FSC® C084699

dedication

For Wallace and Edna McAfee who wrote this
book on my heart four decades ago.

acknowledgements

It is now cliché to say that it takes a community to write a book. Nonetheless, it remains true. My first thanks goes to those who have opened their hearts, become vulnerable and explored Transformational Inquiry with me over the years. This book is as much theirs as mine, for I only wrote down what they taught me.

In a similar vein, I recently led a training session for Transformational Inquiry facilitators. During our few days together, they managed to turn all my plans upside down and reorient my understanding of this work. They helped shift it from an adaptation of Kegan and Lahey's Immunity to Change to a process of its own that is grounded in ancient spiritual wisdom. So, thanks to Jan and Gerhard Bihl, Bonnie Bates, Jenifer Manlowe, Laurel Andrews and Ted Reeve. Also, a special thanks to Amy Nolet for her essential contributions.

Of course, my heartfelt thanks to Robert Kegan and Lisa Lahey for creating such a revolutionary tool and for their encouragement, and to Ken Wilber for his ongoing support of my work.

Last, and certainly not least, are the folks who helped put this book into coherent form: my editor, Catherine Exton, and my publisher, Keith Bellamy. Without them it would still be scattered around my office.

Much Love to you all . . . Tom

table of contents

acknowledgements iv

foreword.. xii

introduction 1
    The Big Picture 2
    The Small Picture 4
    The Smaller Picture 5
    An Audacious Claim.. 7
    What Is Consciousness? 8
    What is Crazy Wisdom?.. 9
    The Plan for this Book 11

part one: foundation.. 14

chapter 1: immunity to change.................................... 15
    The Modern Story 16
    The Mechanics of Immunity to Change......................... 20
    Working with Big Assumptions 26

chapter 2: the faith setting 28
    It's All about Attitude! 28
    Challenges for Traditional Faith Communities.................. 29
    Opportunities for Traditional Faith Communities............. 32
    Emerging Faith Communities 34

chapter 3: a multitude of cosmologies 35

Cosmology I: The World is Made of Stories 37
Cosmology II: Sophia Perennis 39
Cosmology III: The New Science 41
Cosmology IV: Neuropsychology—
Rewiring the Material Brain 44
Cosmology V: The Law of Three 45
Cosmology VI: Christian Journeys of Awakening 47
    Map 1: The Liturgical Year 47
    Map 2: The Gospel of Thomas 48

part two: the crazy wisdom tools of transformational inquiry 50

chapter 4: first steps 51

Don't Fix It! 52
A Spiritual Frame 54
Tools for Daily Practice 54
Whining Our Way into Nobility (Discovering
a Noble Commitment) 55
A Spiritual Frame 57
Tools for Daily Practice 57
Damn! Not again! (Undermining Behaviors) 58
Tools for Daily Practice 58
I Really Did Mean to Hurt You (Accepting
Just the Right Amount of Responsibility) 59
A Spiritual Frame 61
Tools for Daily Practice 61

chapter 5: hidden motivations 63

What, Me Worry? (Liberating Anxieties) 63
Where Did You Come From? (Uncovering
our Competing Commitments) 64
A Spiritual Frame 66
Tools for Daily Practice 66
Getting to Know You (Interviewing
Our Competing Commitments) 67
Instructions 67
Taking the Role of the Noble Commitment 68
Taking the Role of the Competing Commitment 68

A Spiritual Frame 69
Tools for Daily Practice 70
Falling In Love Again (The Practice of Psychodrama) 70
Round 1: Release 71
Round 2: Justifying our Competing Commitments 72
Round 3: Forgiveness 74
A Spiritual Frame 76
Tools for Daily Practice 76

chapter 6: into the depths **78**
Diving in! (Uncovering Big Assumptions) 79
A Spiritual Frame 80
Tools for Daily Practice 81
The Elephant's in Charge (Our Big Assumptions in Action) 81
A Spiritual Frame 83
Tools for Daily Practice 83
Long Ago and Far Away (Writing the History
    of our Big Assumptions) 83
A Spiritual Frame 84
Tools for Daily Practice 84
Check it Out! (Safe Tests) 85
Iterative Safe Tests 85
Natural Safe Tests 86
A Spiritual Frame 86
Tools for Daily Practice 87
They're Only Thoughts! 87
A Spiritual Frame 88
Tools for Daily Practice 88
I Ain't Goin' There! (Writing into Fear) 89
A Spiritual Frame 89
Tools for Daily Practice 90
Is It True? (The Work of Byron Katie) 90
Turnarounds 91
John's Turnarounds 93
A Spiritual Frame 95
Tools for Daily Practice 95

chapter 7: this too shall pass **97**
Round 1: Somatic ITC 97

Round 2: This Too Shall Pass 100
A Spiritual Frame 101
Tools for Daily Practice 102

chapter 8: the whole shebang 103

Week 1: Beginning 103
Week 2: The Shift from Commitments to Behaviors 105
Week 3: The Shift from Behaviors to
Worries and Competing Commitments 107
Week 4: Getting To Know Our Competing Commitments......109
Week 5: From Competing
Commitments to Big Assumptions.................................109
Week 6—Week 8 (or beyond): Falling in
Love Again (Psychodrama) 110
Week 9 (or so): Check it Out! (Safe Tests) 111
Week 10: They're Only Thoughts and I Ain't Goin' There! 112
Week 11: Review and Renewal 114
Week 12+: Is It True? (The Work of Byron Katie) 114
Week 14: This Too Shall Pass...115

appendix a: theoretical foundations
of transformational inquiry 116

The Big Picture 117
Quadrants 117
Lines of Development...118
Stages of Development...119
States of Consciousness...121
Types..122
The Theoretical Foundations of Immunity to Change 122
Three Plateaus in Adult Mental Complexity..........................123
The Socialized Mind..123
The Self-Authoring Mind...123
The Self-Transforming Mind 124
Technical versus Adaptive Change...125
A Dynamic Immune System 125
Subject/Object Relations 126

appendix b: summary of tools 129

Don't Fix It! 130

Whining Our Way into Nobility (Discovering
  a Noble Commitment)..130
Damn! Not again! (Undermining Behaviors) 130
I Really Did Mean to Hurt You (Accepting
  Just the Right Amount of Responsibility) 130
What, Me Worry? (Liberating Anxieties)
  and Where Did You Come From?
  (Uncovering our Competing Commitments) 131
Getting to Know You (Interviewing
  Our Competing Commitments)..131
Falling In Love Again (The Practice of Psychodrama) 131
Diving in! (Uncovering Big Assumptions)..........................131
The Elephant's in Charge (Our Big Assumptions in Action) ...132
Long Ago and Far Away (Writing the History
  of our Big Assumptions)...132
Check it Out! (Safe Tests) 132
They're Only Thoughts! 132
I Ain't Goin' There! (Writing into Fear) 132
Is It True? (The Work of Byron Katie)................................133
Somatic ITC..133

**appendix c: examples of completed
  four-column worksheets................................... 134**
Example 1. On Becoming Sexually Attractive 135
Example 2. On Being Ignored 136
Example 3. On Being Right 137
Example 4. On Weight Loss 138
Example 5. On Becoming a More Confident Presenter 139
Example 6. On Not Being in Control 140

**appendix d: extended transcript
  of a psychodrama 141**
Transcript...142
Review of Noble and Competing Commitments...................142
Begin Psychodrama..144
Round 1: Catharsis...144
Round 2: Justifying Our Competing Commitments 148
Round 3: Forgiveness 152

appendix e: byron katie worksheets 157

Worksheet 1: Judge-Your-Neighbor Worksheet 158
Worksheet 2: One-Belief-at-a-Time Worksheet 159

endnotes **160**

about the author.. **v**

foreword

For nearly three decades I have been trying to help clergy, faith communities and even denominations find ways to transition their traditional religious institutions into contemporary faith expressions. The hope is they might survive the enormous social changes already happening in the western world. I did not do this to save institutional churches necessarily or even Christianity as most people understand it. I did it, and continue to do so, because I seriously believe genuine faith communities are uniquely positioned to foster a real shift in consciousness the world so desperately needs today. I attempted to do this first by creating a new faith community model as a pastor. Years later I traveled all over the country doing church growth workshops in hundreds of churches. Ten years ago I took over the reins of a non-profit organization that has been devoted to modernizing churches by dealing with everything from theology to creating different models for spiritual communities.

It is not easy to look back over the amount of time, energy and money I expended in these efforts and accept the reality I probably influenced very little significant change. Change of any kind is hard for the majority of us. We like our patterns. We are more comfortable with our walls of familiarity. Significant change can be outright painful for many people. Religious communities have even greater roadblocks for change than other institutions. They are frankly designed to resist change. They are usually bound by ancient creeds, outdated belief systems and Holy documents that cannot be challenged. And for many there is often the spoken and unspoken fear of infinite retribution.

And maybe just as importantly, long term supporters frequently do not want their faith communities to change. In our rapidly changing world, churches can be one of the few places left that remain the same for them. So many people find comfort in reciting the creeds they may have been declaiming since childhood. They find familiarity in hearing divinely inspired texts but give little thought to the complexities of biblical contradiction. They love the ancient traditions simply because they are traditional. And yes there is the familiar music accompanied by the pipe organ that brings back fond memories for many. But every year there are fewer people for whom these traditions are familiar or even comforting.

The only clear thing that seems to be changing in churches today is the falling number of people who attend services on Sundays. In the last 50 years, most denominations have lost about one percent of the membership annually. In the 30 years I have been consulting churches on change, it is estimated that over 100,000 churches have closed. Today depending on whose statistics you want to use, churches all over the country are closing at a rate of somewhere between 4,000 to 7,000 churches a year. Southern Baptist researcher, Thom Rainer, in a recent article entitled *13 Issues for Churches in 2013*" puts the estimate higher. He believes between 8,000 and 10,000 churches will likely close in a given year.

I have talked about these statistics with denominational leaders, influential clergy, presidents of seminaries and scholars for decades. Nothing significant seems to change. The mantra for years has been, "Oh, they will come back when they have children." For the vast majority of young adults today there is no coming back. Well over 60 percent of young adults have never been in a church, a synagogue or a temple. They have little or no religious experience and what they have had tends to be viewed as a negative.

So you can imagine how surprised I was when I met Tom Thresher for coffee over eight years ago. I had heard about the unique church in Washington State he was leading. I looked him up to see what he was doing that was so different. Not only was Tom aware of the troubling statistics and the roadblocks to change in our faith communities but he also has been looking for new ways to break the impasse. We both had given a great deal of thought to the situation and we began to share some of our ideas about how to implement change. The friendship and those conversations have continued on a regular basis since that day.

As a former businessman, and a theologian, I tended to think in terms promoting a new Christian message that might be more attractive to our younger and better educated generations. But Tom is a trained educator. He looked more closely at the possibility of changing the way participants think through spiritual education rather than just trying to update the Christian message. Let's call it **Christianity 2014**. We both agreed any significant change was only going to happen through better education and meaningful and intimate conversations. Our goals were similar. I thought we should develop better curriculum for theological investigation. Tom was clear that real change is not possible without personal work which can only happen in small groups. This requires a well thought out plan and tools to break the impasses. This is what one will find in this his latest book, **Crazy Wisdom.**

Building around the revolutionary work of Harvard psychologists Robert Kegan and Lisa Lahey called **Immunity to Change**, Tom has designed a process for participants in small groups to develop a new, expansive awareness. Using this process, individuals and eventually communities, are able to make important changes while developing the greater mental and emotional complexity required in today's world.

Tom makes the audacious claim here that faith communities are uniquely situated to lead the evolution of human consciousness to help create a more just, caring and sustainable world. **Crazy Wisdom** is dedicated to answering how we just might go about doing that.

Tom brings a dozen years of practice in his faith community to the table and a lot of valuable research. He has developed a wide variety of tools to help folks nudge their awareness into more expansive realms. The tools are described and set within different spiritual cosmologies to connect them to a larger context. There are practices for daily use and a basic curriculum is provided. Not surprisingly, these tools are grounded in humanity's great wisdom traditions.

I close with this warning. This book does not offer a silver bullet or simple fix for our dying faith communities. It has nothing to do with the length of sermons or what kind of music we should have in our congregations. It is not about moving the pews or adding coffee tables in the sanctuary. It is not about church renewal.

It is about doing something new and it is not going to be simple for a lot of people. It is about changing the way we learn, the way we think and the way we relate. It is about going deeper than most people are used to going in our competitive, goal driven society. The book is designed for those in small groups who sincerely want to dive more deeply into the profound wisdom of their traditions to make essential personal changes in their lives through a growing awareness. I feel confident this book could provide the model and the foundation for a small group program wherever and however they are formed. It may also fill the needs of the thousands of people who contact our offices every year, searching for a spiritual community with a small group program or for those who want to form their own small group. Providing them with such an opportunity may be one of the most important things we can do today.

Fred Plumer
Progressive Christianity.org

introduction

How wonderful that we have met with a paradox. Now
we have some hope of making progress.
Niels Bohr

"May you live in interesting times." Whether this is a blessing or a curse, it is clear we live in interesting, if not unprecedented times. The global challenges we confront may threaten humanity's very existence. If this is true, then what can we do? Crazy Wisdom tells us that evolving our consciousness will help. Perhaps, then, this book is about saving the world, very . . . very . . . slowly.

In the following pages I present a variety of paradoxical tools called Transformational Inquiry (or Inquiry, for short). These are contemporary tools derived from core insights of the great wisdom traditions. They can be used by anyone, but are especially powerful when used in small, facilitated groups. My methods are grounded in ancient spiritual (not religious) practices like mindfulness, forgiveness, surrender, not-knowing, shadow work, accepting impermanence, empathy, and confronting fear. Because of this orientation, faith communities offer ideal settings for these practices. By faith community I mean any group engaged in issues of ultimate concern, meaning-making, life purpose, what really matters, awakening and so on. This definition can encompass everything from traditional religious institutions to informal study groups. But these tools are not limited to the faith setting. Any group desiring to engage in personal and collective transformation will be well served by these methods.

Most people will not use all of the tools presented here. My hope is that you, and members of your community, will find a few tools that you can incorporate into your daily activities. If practiced as an easy part of your daily life, they will expand the horizons of your understanding, deepen your capacity for caring, and open you to greater awareness of presence.

Let's look at why these tools are important today.

THE BIG PICTURE

In his book, *The Future*, former Vice-President Al Gore postulates that

> There is a clear consensus that the future now emerging will be extremely different from anything we have ever known in the past. It is a difference not of degree but of kind. There is no prior period of change that remotely resembles what humanity is about to experience. We have gone through revolutionary periods of change before, but none as powerful or as pregnant with the fraternal twins—peril and opportunity—as the ones that are beginning to unfold. Nor have we ever experienced so many revolutionary changes unfolding simultaneously and converging with one another.[1]

Gore identifies six fundamental forces creating a world unlike any we have known before:

1. the emergence of a deeply interconnected global economy,
2. a "Global Mind" created by our planet-wide communications,
3. a new balance of political power,
4. the emergence of rapid, unsustainable growth,
5. a new set of biological, biochemical, genetic, and materials science technologies that are reweaving the fabric of life itself, and
6. a radical new relationship between human civilization and the earth's basic ecological systems.[2]

According to the ancient philosopher, Sophocles, "Nothing vast enters the life of mortals without a curse." Each driver of global change is vast and begets both blessings and curses. These drivers are transforming our world, whether we want them to or not. They certainly feel overwhelming! But overwhelming or not, we must respond. The question is how?

The sociobiologist Rebecca Costa offers a helpful framing in her book *The Watchman's Rattle*. Costa argues that civilizations collapse because they reach a cognitive threshold, a level of complexity that overwhelms the mental capacity of the population. A cognitive threshold occurs naturally in every society because our brains evolve slowly while societies change rapidly. "Consequently, the difference between an advanced culture that survives and one that does not may simply boil down to whether a society develops new ways to triumph over a naturally reoccurring cognitive threshold."[3]

Harvard psychologist, Robert Kegan, quantified a similar observation twenty years ago in his classic text, *In Over Our Heads, The Mental Demands of Modern Life*. Kegan's data indicated that less than 50 percent of the American population constructs the mental complexity adequate for our modern world; and 20 percent or fewer are ready for the complexities of postmodern society.[4] We are truly in over our heads.

Costa points to two indicators that show a society is approaching a cognitive threshold. The first is gridlock. "Gridlock occurs when civilizations become unable to comprehend or resolve large, complex problems, despite acknowledging beforehand that these issues may lead to their demise."[5] Instead of solving our issues, we kick them down the road to the next generation.

The second indicator is the "substitution of beliefs for knowledge and fact." We thrive when knowledge and belief exist side by side and neither dominates our life. But knowledge and beliefs disconnect under complex situations:

> Suddenly, water we once fetched directly from our well comes from a faucet, and we no longer can discern where it originates, how it was processed, distributed, priced or allocated. The same goes for our monetary system, laws, taxes, satellite television, and terrorism. Every aspect of life accelerates in complexity. Not only does the number of things we must comprehend grow, the intricacy of these things also exponentially increases. So, the amount of knowledge our brains must acquire to achieve real understanding quickly becomes overwhelming.[6]

When we are overwhelmed by the complexity of information confronting us we quite naturally fall back upon assumptions, beliefs and unproven ideas about our existence.

Costa argues that "once a society begins exhibiting the first two signs—gridlock and the substitution of beliefs for facts—the stage is set for collapse."[7] That's the bad news. The good news is that "the signs of a cognitive threshold begin appearing long before collapse, so there is ample time to act."

The subtitle of Costa's book, *Thinking Our Way Out of Extinction*, indicates both its brilliance and its limitation. The limitation is that it focuses on cognition, and we know that thinking is only one of the intelligences we bring to deciding and acting. Thought, nonetheless, is an essential (and often leading) dimension in confronting complex change. Neuroscientists are discovering that our brain is evolving to engage this change. According to Costa, in addition to the left side of our brain that analyses, and the right side that synthesizes, "today we have evidence of a third, heretofore-unknown cognitive process called insight, a faculty uniquely designed for highly demanding, complex problems."[8]

With the word *insight* Costa points to a way of knowing (an epistemology) that exceeds rationality. The question is, How do we develop this new way of knowing? In other words, how do we evolve consciousness to meet the demands of a changing world? Crazy Wisdom is part of the answer.

. But the Crazy Wisdom tools of Transformational Inquiry don't just apply to global issues. As the next two sections highlight, these tools have a particular applicability to the great questions of our personal life, as well as to the mundane frustrations we face daily. The Small Picture accentuates the need for these tools as each of us ferrets out our life's meaning and purpose.

THE SMALL PICTURE

"Screw enlightenment," she screamed "I just want to feel better now! I don't care about some imaginary time when I'll wake up and all my problems will be over! I want to stop hurting now!"

"But . . . but . . . but . . . enlightenment is the answer to all our problems. When you wake up, your ego goes away. Bam, just like that! And all your problems are solved. Who doesn't want enlightenment?"

"Stop! I've heard this crap a thousand times! 'Just wake up and then it'll all be perfect,'" she says with a sneer. "But what are the chances I'll have this total awakening thing? One in a million? One in a billion? Even if I do wake up, any decent teacher will tell you it's just the beginning; you still gotta deal with all the crap from your old self. Waking up's got nothing for me! I hurt now. I need to know what I can do when I get all snarled up in my head. I want to know how to deal with rejection. How do I stop making the same mistakes over and over and over again? I want something I can use now to free my mind from all this confusion! If you can't give me that, then get the hell out of the way!"

"But that's what enlightenment brings!" he implores. "Your mistakes become irrelevant. Your thoughts go away so you can't get snarled in your head. It all gets clear and you live in perfect bliss!"

"I just want a good life" she says, close to tears (and ready to strangle him). "I want the normal things, enough money to get by, a loving partner, kids perhaps. And I don't want to be stressed all the time! I don't want to complain all the time

or long for some past glory. I just want to be happy. But I don't know where to start (tears running down her cheeks). My dumb-ass spiritual friends tell me 'wake up and it'll all be fine.' My church tells me to believe some crap that doesn't make any sense! And the media says 'buy, buy, buy' and you'll be happy. Won't anybody give me some straight talk?"

We all want to save the world, but it's a terribly abstract endeavor. Mostly we want to feel better (now please!). Just like this young woman who has become disillusioned with the idea of enlightenment, most of us just want to be happy. How do we find happiness? Crazy Wisdom offers surprisingly effective tools. But sometimes, what we want is far more mundane than life purpose, or finding happiness. Sometimes, we just want to make some small change in our lives as the Smaller Picture highlights.

THE SMALLER PICTURE

Ya know, I really wanted to do it differently this time! I swore I wouldn't blow up at Billy for leaving the milk on the counter. It's so stupid! Why should I get tweaked because he left the damn milk on the counter? But I did! I walked into the kitchen, saw the milk, and started yelling at him! He started to cry—he's only six for God's sake—and here's his mom screaming at him for nothing. I'm so sick of this, but I just don't know how to change!

But then again, what if I didn't get mad when he left the milk out? All kinds of horrible things could happen! The milk would probably go bad. Bobby might grow up to be irresponsible, a real slacker! He's gotta be responsible now! It's a slippery slope and before you know it he won't be getting his homework in on time, he'll fail his classes and flunk out of school! He'll be a bum on the street and everyone will know what a lousy mom I am! They won't want anything to do with me and I'll have a washed-out druggie to care for me in my old age.

. . .

Damn! Stuck behind idiots again! Why are they going 25 in a 35 mile zone? This is no time for a Sunday drive; it's the middle of the week for Christ's sake! I'm in a hurry! Hey, maybe I can get around them now. Damn! Double lines. Not enough passing room! Arrrggghh!"

Okay relax. Remember, you're not on a schedule! You're just going to the gym. You don't have to be there at any particular time. But they're still in my way! All right! I can pass! "SOBs, get out of the way!" I yell as I race by.

"O, shit! Did it again! I got all worked up over nothing. I was really going to change this time (really)! I was going to remind myself that I wasn't in a hurry and just chill out. Screwed up again! I'll never get it right!"

. . .

Oh, I'm always so anxious! I worry about everything! I want to meditate or do something to help me relax. But every time I start I get caught up in my thoughts and never get good enough to get some relief. Why I can't change?

My life feels so meaningless! I remember when I was a child and I went to church with my parents. I got this wonderful feeling, like I was safe and everything was OK. I'd like to feel like that again. But I don't even look for a place. I don't get it!

My neighbor just asked me to help with a local school project. I came up with some lame excuse for why I couldn't help out. I feel so guilty! I'd like to help out but when the opportunity arises, I always seem to say "No." Why am I so selfish?

Sometimes, we just want to make a small change. We want to alter some small detail of our life to make it better. But how? Again, the Crazy Wisdom of Transformational Inquiry offers surprisingly powerful tools.

The Big Picture, The Small Picture, and The Smaller Picture look different at first glance, but at the core, they bear a striking similarity. Every story is driven by a set of invisible assumptions and Core Beliefs that repudiate our most heartfelt desire to do better. In none of these scenarios does doing better require new skills; each demands a new way of knowing. Each requires that we *grow up* the assumptions that run our lives.

That said, this is not a self-help book or a book about social change. It is a book for individuals and small groups wanting to lead the evolution of human consciousness during our time of great need. These are practical tools for penetrating the invisible stories that run our lives and keep us stuck . . . and how we can change them.

Crazy Wisdom and tools of Transformational Inquiry are about making little changes that lead to big results. Buckminster Fuller stressed the importance of small changes with his metaphor of the "trim tab."[9] The trim tab is a small rudder along the edge of the large rudder that turns a big ship. Immense energy is required to turn the giant rudder that steers a ship; but with comparatively little energy, applied judiciously, a small rudder can move the large rudder that steers an ocean liner. Similarly, small changes in the Core Beliefs that run our lives can have huge impacts on our actions in the world. When small groups and communities work together to make small, fundamental changes in their individual and collective hidden assumptions, great things can happen. Small groups, engaging Crazy Wisdom through the tools of Inquiry, can become the trim tabs for profound social and individual change.

An Audacious Claim

As both a Christian minister and an ordained Integral Minister[10], let me advocate doing this work in traditional faith communities with an audacious claim: faith communities, particularly churches, can, and should, *lead the evolution of human consciousness to create a wiser, more caring and sustainable world*. These faith communities possess some truly unique resources for evolving consciousness. (Again, if you are not part of a faith community and want to use these tools in an entirely secular setting, you will be pleased with the results.)

First, established faith communities can provide settings that are judiciously balanced between support and challenge to create what Kegan and Lahey call "optimum tension." Western cultures give faith communities license to transform people at the level of their soul. As institutions, these communities work to create deep trust and caring. When this trust and caring is balanced with appropriate challenges, they provide an essential prerequisite for deep evolutionary change. While this is no longer the exclusive domain of churches and such (in part because they have failed to provide the kind of spiritual transformation people are seeking) traditional faith communities nonetheless retain preeminent cultural authority to influence individual perspectives on life, meaning, and relationships. I know of no better institutional framework for nurturing the evolution of consciousness.

Second, faith communities, particularly churches, *own* the great cultural myths of our societies from which we construct our identities.[11] Whether you were raised Christian or not, if you grew up in the West you were saturated with the values, ideals, ethics and priorities of Christianity. Christianity establishes the ground from which we create our personal meaning-making stories. In that sense, we in the West all grew up Christians.

The great stories of forgiveness, caring, love, sacrifice, courage and faith belong to the established faith communities. Only these communities have the authority to interpret and enlarge them. Only faith communities have the legitimacy to adapt, modify, translate and expand our foundational stories to create a space where individuals can increase the complexity of their minds, the compassion of their hearts and the *unknowing* of their spirits. Indeed, it is the responsibility of faith communities to give this to the culture.

Finally, established religious communities have a truly rare commodity in our fast-paced, world: *time*. Faiths don't produce widgets.[12] While all institutions have to deal with finances, these faith communities don't have corporate boards looking over their shoulders demanding quarterly returns on investment. They have God's time, if you will. Faith communities offer a rare refuge, a place where individuals can take the time to evolve.

Personally, I would hate to see us waste such precious cultural resources, but we might. The idea of faith communities, especially churches, leading folks into new, more expansive modes of consciousness seems absurd in the West. The public face of faith, especially Christianity, is of some fanatical preacher selling retrograde ideas to a gullible populace. This image prevents many people from even entering a faith community, especially a church. But the deep human yearning for something greater remains, and perhaps some churches will take up the challenge. For these bold explorers, chapter 2 outlines the challenges and opportunities available to traditional religious communities using Transformational Inquiry.

What Is Consciousness?

I claim that the Crazy Wisdom tools of Transformation Inquiry can help evolve human consciousness which, in turn, will help us confront global change, be happier, and make personal changes. But what is this consciousness that is evolving?

Consciousness is literally the context in which everything unfolds, it is the Infinite. Similarly, personal consciousness is the context in which your life unfolds. More specifically,

> Consciousness is the quality or state of awareness, or, of being aware of an external object or something within oneself. It has been defined as: sentience, awareness, subjectivity, the ability to experience or to feel, wakefulness, having a sense of selfhood, and the executive control system of the mind. Despite the difficulty in definition, many philosophers believe that there is a broadly–shared, underlying intuition about what consciousness is. As Max Velmans and Susan Schneider wrote in *The Blackwell Companion to Consciousness*, "Anything that we are aware of at a given moment forms part of our consciousness, making conscious experience at once the most familiar and most mysterious aspect of our lives."[13]

Good enough for our purposes. If consciousness is a quality or state of awareness, then how does it evolve? According to Harvard developmental psychologists Robert Kegan and Lisa Lahey, whose work provides the scaffolding for the Crazy Wisdom tools of Transformational Inquiry, we can say consciousness evolves when that which was *subject* to us becomes an *object* to the next level of our development. (See Appendix A for a discussion of these terms.) This simply means that whenever the set of lenses (the paradigm) I am observing the world through becomes something I can look at and operate on then my consciousness evolves.

This is important, and simpler than these sentences suggest. We do not see the world as it is. We see it through the beliefs and the assumptions, the hopes and dreams, the fears and anxieties we have constructed over our lifetime. These, in turn, create a set of filters that make the world meaningful to us. These filters explain the world, tell us what is important or dangerous, show us where we belong, and construct our identities. These filters are invisible to us because we are looking through them, just as we would look through a pair of well-fitting glasses that have become invisible to our awareness. We say they are *subject*, as in subjective, because we are not aware of them. In Kegan's language, *"they have us."*

When we can look at our beliefs, assumptions, fears and anxieties as if they were something sitting on the table in front of us, we say they have become an *object*. They no longer have us, *we have them*, in the sense that we can now question them and act to change them, at least in some minor way.[14]

Again, consciousness evolves when that which was subject (invisible to our awareness) becomes an object of our awareness that we can see and act upon. This is consistent with the ancient spiritual insight that states *whatever is brought out of darkness into the light of awareness is transformed.* And to repeat, consciousness has the best opportunity to evolve in a setting that is judiciously balanced between support and challenge, whether that setting is a faith community or a small group of secular practitioners.

WHAT IS CRAZY WISDOM?

I have borrowed the term *Crazy Wisdom* from the Buddhist tradition because it aptly describes the paradoxical nature of the tools I develop here. To borrow from Chögyam Trungpa's book entitled *Crazy Wisdom*:

> Instead we explore further and further and further without looking for an answer. [...] We don't make a big point or an answer out of any one thing. For example, we might think that because we have discovered one particular thing that is wrong with us, that must be *it*, that must be the problem, that must be the answer. No. We don't fixate on that, we go further. "Why is that the case?" We look further and further.

We ask: "Why is this so?" Why is there spirituality? Why is there awakening? Why is there this moment of relief? Why is there such a thing as discovering the pleasure of spirituality? Why, why, why?" We go on deeper and deeper and deeper and deeper, until we reach the point where there is no answer.[15]

Transformational Inquiry has an orientation similar to Trungpa's. His idea, translated into Americanese is, **Don't Fix It!** The Westernized practices of Transformational Inquiry are made up of a variety of counterintuitive, paradoxical methods designed to gently challenge your established sense of reality, that is, the reality you see through the filters constructed by your beliefs, assumptions and fears. The tools offered here are presented in contemporary form, but they derive from our species' most ancient insights. They only appear crazy in the context of contemporary Western society. The tools of Transformational Inquiry mirror the paradoxical orientation of Crazy Wisdom:

Judgments reveal nobility.
Blame inspires hope.
Fear will set you free.
You always lose the war with your mind.
Rationality is a delusion.
What you resist persists.
Doubt everything.
Your body never lies.
Love your enemy . . . really.
And to repeat the granddaddy of them all: DON'T FIX ANYTHING!

Transformational Inquiry attaches trim tabs to the rudder of Core Beliefs that invisibly run our lives. Ironically, the energy to move such a trim tab comes from *curiosity* not intention. When we genuinely inquire, we don't know what answer we will receive or the direction it will take us. This requires faith, the currency of everything from traditional religious communities to spiritual support groups.

THE PLAN FOR THIS BOOK

When I first started writing this book, I thought it would be a simple expansion of the Immunity to Change (ITC) process developed by Kegan and Lahey. As so often happens, the work took on a life of its own and developed its own logic. A major reason is that this work is spiritually (not religiously) oriented. The spiritual setting is very different from the business, government and educational backdrops where Kegan and Lahey have so effectively applied Immunity to Change. As I developed and experimented with these tools, I found that they clearly resonated with a spectrum of sacred stories. When leading Transformational Inquiry, it helps to place the work in a larger, spiritual context. So, in keeping with the insight that our cultural context sets boundaries on the evolution of our personal consciousness, I briefly offer a mixture of sacred cosmologies to contextualize the tools I present. These cosmologies are expansive stories, our great cultural mythologies. They tell us who we are, where we belong, and why we are here. Obviously, I cannot present them with the fullness they deserve. But that is not necessary for our purposes. My goal in offering *a spiritual frame* for the tools of Transformational Inquiry is to encourage you to relate the tools of Inquiry to your tradition, or a variety of traditions.

The tools of Transformational Inquiry emanate from the four-column Immunity to Change process developed by Kegan and Lahey.[16] In the first part of this book, I will introduce you to the mechanics of Immunity to Change set within the context of The Modern Story. The Modern Story is the abiding mythological narrative of the West that answers the questions, *Who are we? Where do we come from?* and *Why are we here?*

My brief exploration of relevant cosmologies introduces the tools of Inquiry and offers a sacred reference point for those tools. When organized in a circle, the four columns of Immunity to Change provide a scaffold for the tools of Transformational Inquiry (see Cosmological Context figure below).The paradoxical tools of Transformational Inquiry reflect Crazy Wisdom and are named accordingly:

- *Whining Our Way into Nobility* reveals the surprising truth behind our complaints.
- *Damn! Not Again!* explores the actions that undercut our most noble desires.
- *I Really Meant to Hurt You* shows us how appropriately accepting blame opens the door to profound change.
- *What, Me Worry?* introduces the remarkable intelligence enfolded in our anxieties.
- *Getting to Know You? helps us* uncover surprising interior selves and discover why we get stuck in behaviors we hate.
- *Falling in Love Again* initiates an internal dialogue grounded in empathy and forgiveness.

- *The Elephant's in Charge!* Brings us face-to-face with the hidden assumptions that run our daily lives.
- *Long Ago and Far Away* reveals the sources of our Core Beliefs.
- *Check It Out* invites us to investigate our core assumptions both observationally and systematically.
- *They're Only Thoughts!* grants permission to derail existing thought patterns.
- *I Ain't Goin' There!* exploits our deepest fears in the service of freedom.
- *Is It True?* uses the disarmingly simple work Byron Katie to *question* the evidence for our most ingrained assumptions.
- *This Too Shall Pass* uses Immunity to Change somatically to embody a pivotal insight.

Finally, chapter 8, The Whole Shebang, integrates these tools into a comprehensive program. Extensive appendices explore the theoretical foundations of Transformational Inquiry and offers transcripts of the more dynamic elements.

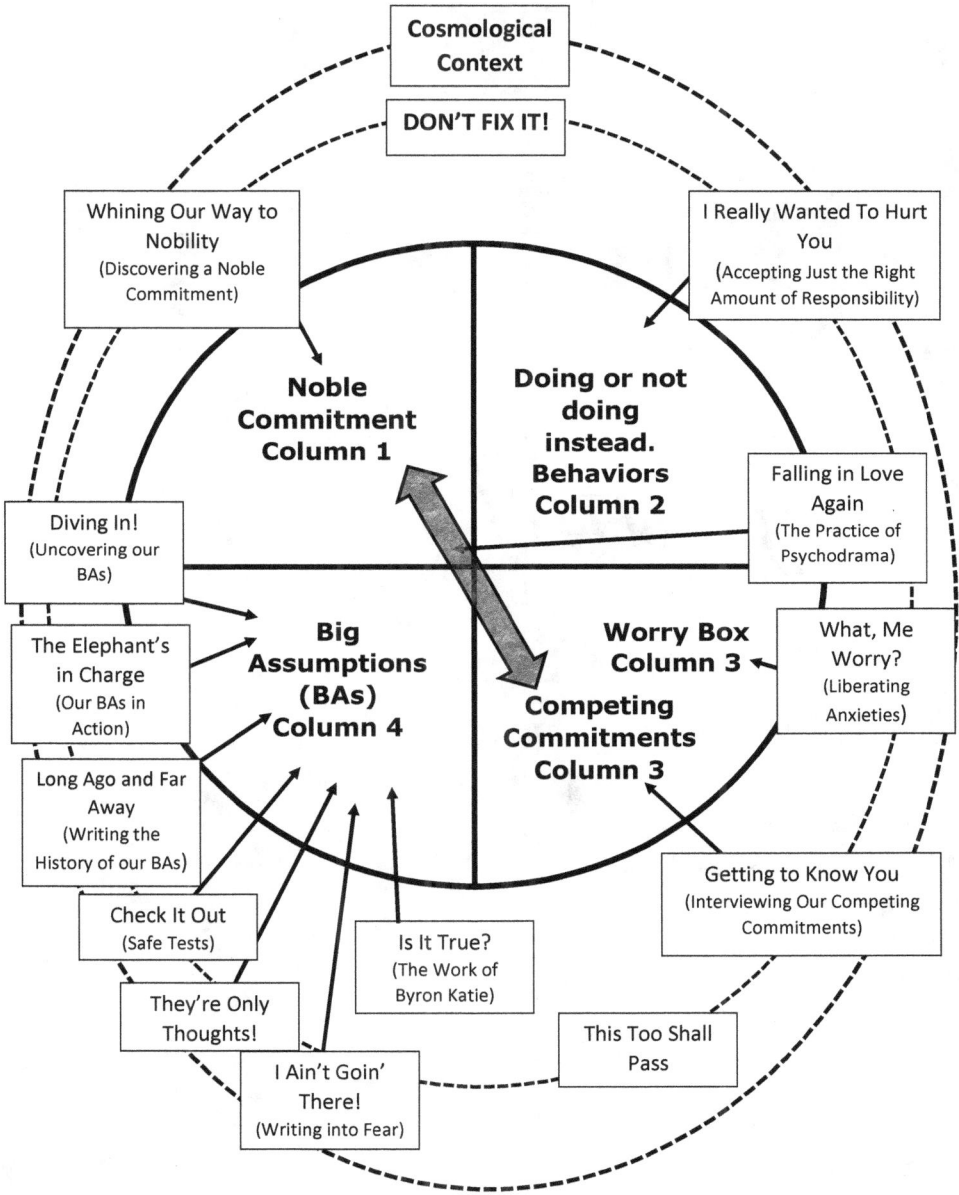

Cosmological Context

DON'T FIX IT!

Whining Our Way to Nobility
(Discovering a Noble Commitment)

I Really Wanted To Hurt You
(Accepting Just the Right Amount of Responsibility)

Noble Commitment Column 1

Doing or not doing instead. Behaviors Column 2

Falling in Love Again
(The Practice of Psychodrama)

Diving In!
(Uncovering our BAs)

The Elephant's in Charge
(Our BAs in Action)

Big Assumptions (BAs) Column 4

Worry Box Column 3

What, Me Worry?
(Liberating Anxieties)

Competing Commitments Column 3

Long Ago and Far Away
(Writing the History of our BAs)

Check It Out
(Safe Tests)

Is It True?
(The Work of Byron Katie)

They're Only Thoughts!

I Ain't Goin' There!
(Writing into Fear)

Getting to Know You
(Interviewing Our Competing Commitments)

This Too Shall Pass

13

part one

foundation

chapter 1

immunity to change

*What do you want and what will you
do to keep from getting it?*
Robert Kegan, Lisa Lahey

In this chapter, I will introduce you to the Immunity to Change process around which Transformational Inquiry builds. It is based on the pioneering work of Harvard developmental psychologists Robert Kegan and Lisa Lahey. A core premise is that we (intentionally or unintentionally) construct and internalize stories of ourselves that form our identities. These internalized stories form our Core Beliefs; Kegan and Lahey call them our Big Assumptions. As these internalized stories change, we change. But our individual stories are never independent of the larger cultural story in which they are enmeshed. A culture's dominant story, or myth, provides the raw material from which each of us constructs a personal story. In turn, our internalized story shapes our behavior. Immunity to Change uncovers our personalized rendition of our culture's dominant myth and challenges it. The dominant myth of the West, from which we construct a personal identity, is the Modern Story.

The Modern Story offers a mostly coherent and interrelated set of assumptions, beliefs, values, and emotions through which we perceive the world around us. We cannot help but perceive through our beliefs and assumptions; seeing the world through our personal set of lenses is intrinsic to human nature. But we don't all perceive through the same set of lenses. Each of us constructs a highly personalized set of beliefs and values through which we engage the world. Still, there are broad similarities across our individual stories that allow categorization. Importantly, for our purposes, our culture promotes a particular spectrum of ideas that provides a coherent cultural context, a myth, from which we each extract bits and pieces to construct our own personal stories of who we are, where we are going, our life's purpose and what will happen when we die.

The Modern Story supplies the primary context in which Kegan and Lahey do most of their work, and is a broad generalization pointing to the common, overlapping and conflicting stories that shape many of the goals of Immunity to Change. This is not a criticism, just the opposite. It is an acknowledgement that the changes needed by most individuals are contextualized by the Modern Story, and Kegan and Lahey lead change where it is dearly needed. The social expectations of the work, educational and governmental environments in which ITC is most commonly applied are deeply grounded in the Modern Story.

THE MODERN STORY

Modernity is a qualitative,
not a chronological, category.
Theodor Adorno

Modernity exalts the virtues of reason, rationality, organization, objectivity and individuality. A champion of the Modern Story might express it as follows:

It has taken a long time, but we've finally overcome irrationality! We no longer believe the foolishness of a sacred, spiritual world. We've finally recognized that we are purely physical, just stuff. So, now we can live our lives in well-organized communities run, for the most part, by effective governments and corporate entities. We can work at jobs that are highly mechanized, organized and efficient. As each of us becomes more productive, we help build a better future. Our free markets guarantee that our individual choices will be heeded and, when organized properly, we can produce more so everyone can hope for a better standard of living than their parents. The new technologies constantly emerging from our scientific understanding of the world make better and better use of our scarce resources and bring us exciting new products. By breaking down and understanding the essential components of this world, we become the masters of nature herself. For the first time, it's possible for us to create a world that meets the needs of all humans. Eventually, our individual and cultural differences will disappear and our motivations for war will be obsolete. It really doesn't get better this!

On a personal level, the Modern Story emphasizes the following.

- The uniqueness of the individual represents his or her essential reality.
- Individuals are or ought to be free.
- Individuals are responsible for their own actions, but only for their own actions.
- An individual's subjective experience of the world is *real* by definition.
- Individuals possess certain rights over and against collectives.
- Individuals are ultimately responsible for creating themselves.[17]

To be a workable cultural myth, the Modern Story must provide the individual with answers to the following questions: Who am I? What is my purpose? Is my life meaningful? Where do I come from? Where do I belong? What will happen when I die?

Based upon the criteria laid out above, two individualized expressions of the Modern Story are presented below. The first story describes someone who perceives him- or herself to be successful within the modern cultural criteria. The second deems him- or herself unsuccessful according to the same story.

STORY ONE

Who am I? I am myself, of course! I am the author of my life. There's nobody like me in the whole universe. I use my unique abilities to plan my life. I look carefully at what I want to achieve, I think about it, I strategize, and I create a plan that will get me to my goals. As I go, I evaluate my plans and adapt them as needed. Of course, I have to make adjustments along the way, but I weigh the benefits and costs and choose the direction that will best get me to my goals. When I make mistakes, or I fail at some endeavors, I pick myself up, reevaluate where I am, develop a new strategy and put it into action.

Lots of things tell me I'm successful. I live in a beautiful home, I drive a new car, my kids are in good schools and they do pretty well. My partner also works as a professional. We have the normal couple problems but we both have capable therapists. We try to engage one another in rational dialogue before exploding into emotions. Most of the time we succeed.

My success is my own! I can't make decisions for anyone else, and I have no patience for those who aren't willing to make the sacrifices that will bring them success. Sure, I've had some help along the way, most of my success is self-generated.

What's my purpose? What makes life meaningful? Well, I want to be as good as I can be. I do my best at work; I'm a loyal and dedicated spouse and parent; I stay in good health; I give back to my society. I know I am alive when, having worked so hard, I finally reach my goal. I feel it my bones . . . I'm truly alive!

You know, we live in the very best system there is. We have a democracy where people can choose what to make out of their lives. If they want to better themselves they can make the sacrifices, get the education, invest wisely, and really live the good life. We live in a country where our efforts are rewarded. Just look at me, I didn't come from wealth or privilege. I had to pull myself up by my bootstraps. I worked hard through school and I listened to those who taught me. I did what I was told to do; I learned and discovered how to make my way. We all have this opportunity. If you don't take advantage of these opportunities it's your own damn fault!

Where do I belong? Where do I come from? The old stories said I come from God or some kind of heavenly realm. That's crap! I went to church when I was young and heard all the stories, but when I grew up I saw they were just fairy tales. I took a really hard look at the world around me and decided that the scientists were right. After all, they were the only ones giving rational, cogent responses to the questions. Science says we're the result of some 14 billion years of evolution, that random chance and survival of the fittest made us who we are today. That really nails it! We've evolved the intelligence to create the world we want, a world where everyone has enough if they'll just work for it.

And what happens when I die? Well, I just die. I'm done, it's over. I'm really nothing more than a bunch of atoms anyway. I know that the neurons in my brain will simply die. If I have any kind of immortality it will be the legacy I leave my children and my grandchildren. I've already passed on my genes to them. Perhaps I can leave them some financial assets that will ease their way as they make their choices. And hopefully, I will live on in their memories. I hope my life will have been an example to them of how they can live, how they can achieve, and how they can give back. My body, my mind, everything about me, returns to dust. And that's fine, if I have lived my life well, thoughtfully and with integrity. If I have made a contribution to the survival of our species, I will have lived a good life.

Of course, not everyone will successfully live out the Modern Story. For many, the Modern Story voices their failure. Even though they are not successful within its parameters, they are nonetheless living it out, as the following story illustrates.

STORY TWO

Who am I? I'm the screw-up, the one making all the bad choices. I can mess up just about anything! I usually think I know what I'm doing, I have grandiose ideas, but they never come out as I plan. I know I can do better, but no matter what I do I screw it up! Maybe I'm just stupid. Maybe something's wrong with me. My friends are successful. They have nice families, kids; they seem to live comfortably. I got into all the same schools. But I just goofed off. Mostly I partied instead of studying. They say I'm living out my choices. But it seems unfair!

Recently, I swore I'd get my act together. I took this workshop on personal motivation. It was great! I came out of there convinced that this time I was going to make my life different. I really worked on it. I looked at what I really wanted to do. I wrote down all the things I had to get done and started doing them. I checked items off one by one and got a lot of them done, but then I kinda lost interest. Somehow, my discipline and motivation just evaporated. Pretty soon I just wasn't going anywhere . . . again.

I'm really impressed with my friends. They make choices and stick with them. I'm amazed they can think through all the things they have to do so logically and rationally . . . and then do it! That sure isn't me. Sometimes, I feel like I just don't fit in this world. I operate off my emotions. If something fun comes up, I just go for it. I don't really think about whether it will further my career or if it's in my life plan. Guess that's why I'm not very successful.

What's my purpose? What gives my life meaning? Geez, I don't really know. I'm not sure I have any purpose, I wonder if my life has any meaning. I'm such a loser! But you know, somebody's got to be a loser so all those other people can feel like winners, right? Now, maybe that's my purpose, to make all those other people look good!

Sometimes I wonder if I really belong here. I'm just not cut out for this world; my brain doesn't work like everybody else's. I go by my gut feelings; I don't think I'm really smart enough to live in this world. But, you know, I do have a lot of friends. Folks just like to hang out with me. They tell me lots of stuff about their personal life, about how unhappy they are, what's going on with their relationships. And I listen, and they seem to feel better. Why isn't that more important?

I don't think much about where I come from or what will happen to me when I die. I suppose the scientists are right, and we evolved from chimps. If that's who we are, and there is no God or heaven or hell or any of that, then I guess when I die, I'll just die. I'll just be done and my life will have been more or less pointless. Ouch! I guess I better come up with some way to get my life together.

As I mentioned, the Modern Story provides the context for much of the work of Immunity to Change. This orientation is reflected in the title of Kegan and Lahey's latest book, *Immunity to Change: How to Overcome It and Unlock the Potential in Yourself and Your Organization*[18]. A modern orientation is, of course, most appropriate to the business, government and educational settings in which Immunity to Change is generally practiced, but ITC is wonderfully adaptable beyond the modern frame, as I will develop in later chapters. Now, let me introduce you to the basic Immunity to Change process.

THE MECHANICS OF IMMUNITY TO CHANGE

At the turn of the millennium, Kegan and Lahey's book, *How the Way We Talk Can Change the Way We Work*[19], introduced the basic process of Immunity to Change. The central question, voiced in their introduction, was "What do you really want and what will you do to keep from getting it?"[20] Nearly a decade later, in *Immunity to Change*[21], they further elaborated the process based on their experience and research over the ensuing years. The remainder of this chapter will outline the basic process that is the centerpiece of Transformational Inquiry[22].

Immunity to Change begins with the simple map below (Figure 1.1). In walking through this map, you will discover the hidden, self-serving Competing Commitments that dynamically prevent your improvement goals from being realized, and the Big Assumptions, or Core Beliefs, that sustain them.

COLUMN 1	COLUMN 2	COLUMN 3	COLUMN 4
NOBLE COMMITMENT (Improvement Goal)	DOING OR NOT DOING INSTEAD	COMPETING COMMITMENTS	BIG ASSUMPTIONS CORE BELIEFS

Figure 1.1: Immunity to Change Map

The process begins with a commitment. It is essential that this commitment, or improvement goal, be important to you. On a scale of one to five, where five is *very* important, the improvement goal should rank at least a four. It must be genuinely important, not just something you think you should change. It should also be something you have control over and can change in significant ways. Finally, it should matter. In business, education and government contexts, it should be significantly related to the person's work.

A typical business improvement goal might be: *I'd like to delegate better*. If you are moving into a higher level of management in a business which requires you to oversee a team of qualified professionals, this is likely to a very important goal, ranking at least a four, perhaps a five. This becomes your Column 1 Noble Commitment, your Improvement Goal. It is a good commitment because it requires you to make a fundamental qualitative change, not merely a technical one.

The next step asks the question, "What am I doing or not doing instead that keeps my improvement goal from being realized?" We are looking for behaviors here, not dispositions. We are asking for concrete behaviors that prevent you from achieving your Column 1 Noble Commitment. This is not the time for deep reflection. It's not about why you act the way you do or what you are going to do about it. We are asking a very simple question about actual actions (or lack of action). The more honest you can be the better.

Let's say, for the sake of example, that our manager, rather than delegate, jumps in and does the job herself, or she micromanages the process, or she over-explains. These are recorded in Column 2 (see Figure 1.2).

COLUMN 1	COLUMN 2	COLUMN 3	COLUMN 4
NOBLE COMMITMENT (Improvement Goal)	DOING OR NOT DOING INSTEAD	COMPETING COMMITMENTS	BIG ASSUMPTIONS CORE BELIEFS
My goal is to delegate more effectively.	• Rather than wait, I just do the job on my own. • I get in the middle of everything and micromanage the process. • I over-explain.		

Figure 1.2: Examples of Columns 1 and 2

There is nothing revolutionary about the process thus far. Our manager has identified an improvement goal and discovered the actions that keep her from fulfilling that goal. The rational choice would be to simply change behavior by waiting longer, not micromanaging, or over-explaining. In other words, *just stop it!* But this is a fundamental mistake that guarantees failure. She is using a New-Year's-resolution-strategy based on a heart-felt commitment that is almost certain to fail. The problem is that she is trying to solve an *adaptive* challenge with a *technical* solution. A technical change requires learning a new set of well-understood skills, while an adaptive change demands a new way of knowing.[23]

Moving beyond Column 2, the Immunity to Change process becomes truly revolutionary. Instead of trying to devise new strategies, our manager will use the counterproductive behaviors she has identified in Column 2 to enter into a deeper understanding of herself and engage in a transformative kind of learning. This takes us to Column 3.

You will notice in Figure 1.3 (below) that we have added a *Worry Box* to Column 3. We are going to use the Worry Box to help our manager take something invisible and make it visible. Because we human beings are complex, we abound with commitments. Many of these are noble and desirable, like those in Column 1. Other commitments appear childish and egocentric and can lead to behaviors that thwart the Column 1 Commitments we hold in such high esteem. As Kegan and Lahey stress, we don't have our Column 3 commitments, they *have us!* Since Column 3 is often the hardest step to take in this process, we break it into two half- steps.

The first half-step is to consider doing *the opposite* of each Column 2 behavior and notice what anxieties arise. These anxieties can run from a minor discomfort, to a sense of loss, to fear, to outright terror.

In this example, the manager's goal is to delegate more effectively, but instead of delegating tasks, she micromanages the process. We ask her, then, to imagine *not* micromanaging at all. We ask her to envision staying out of the process entirely. What kinds of anxieties arise for her? She reports that when she imagines staying out of the process, her hands begin to perspire, her heart beats faster, and she gets very anxious. When asked what is going on, she blurts out, "They'll do it all wrong! I'm terrified! If I don't control the process it'll be slaughtered and I'll look stupid!" Her responses are recorded in the Worry Box.

It's one thing to identify fears and anxieties; it's another to own them. And even more than own them, to recognize that our fears are grounded in heartfelt self-protective Commitments, commitments that are as fervently held as our noble Column 1 Commitments. These are not what we generally think of as *commitments*; we consider them to be *defects*, or *character flaws*. They are not aspects of ourselves we want to shout about from the rooftops. But they are part of all of us! In fact, if the self-protective Competing Commitments we derive from our worries embarrass us or make us cringe, then it's likely we're on the right track. Then we are unearthing some deep, self-serving commitments that we normally try to keep hidden, both from ourselves and from others.

Our manager's self-protective, hidden Commitments emerge directly from her Worry Box: *I am committed to having everything perfect* and *I am committed to never looking stupid!* These are powerful Competing Commitments. They follow directly from the fear articulated in the Worry Box; they are self-protective, and they evoke a potent awareness. Her Immunity to Change system emerges! For every unfulfilled Column 1 commitment there is a hidden Competing Commitment (Column 3) preventing it from happening. Her Immunity to Change system is accurately named an *immune system* because when a Column 1 commitment activates a hidden, self-protective Commitment (Column 3) she acts to maintain her balance through her Column 2 behavior. When we look closely, we discover the Column 2 behaviors she perceives as thwarting her noble aspirations are actually brilliant strategies to protect her from some danger perceived through the lens of her Column 3 Competing Commitments. Furthermore, her Immunity to Change is dynamic; the harder she pushes to fulfill her goals (Column 1) the more she threatens her hidden, Competing Commitments, and the more likely they are to undercut her highest aspirations.

This is why will power fails. We're directing our energy to the wrong place! We look for what is wrong with us, but instead discover powerful

Commitments working to maintain the status quo. The Column 2 behaviors that frustrate our Column 1 aspirations are superb strategies for preventing Column 3 disasters from happening. This dynamic is indicated by the arrows in Figure 1.3.

COLUMN 1	COLUMN 2	COLUMN 3	COLUMN 4
NOBLE COMMITMENT (Improvement Goal)	DOING OR NOT DOING INSTEAD	COMPETING COMMITMENTS	BIG ASSUMPTIONS CORE BELIEFS
My goal is to delegate more effectively.	• Rather than wait, I just do the job on my own. • I get in the middle of everything and micromanage the process. • I over-explain.	***Worry Box*** They'll do it all wrong! - I'll look stupid! **Competing Commitments** • I am committed to having everything perfect. • I am committed to never looking stupid.	

Figure 1.3: Dynamic Immunity to Change

While our immune system protects us, it also stifles us. When our Competing Commitments are grounded in fear, they prevent us from living out the life we say we want to live. Our Competing Commitments are grounded in what Kegan and Lahey aptly name Big Assumptions. Our Big Assumptions are the Core Beliefs we hold that are largely invisible to us. They are invisible to us because, as with our Competing Commitments, we don't look *at* them, we look *through* them. Big Assumptions are very much like the eyeglasses we wear to correct our vision. If they are the right prescription, if they are comfortable and don't slide down our noses, we don't notice them. And much like eyeglasses, Big Assumptions fundamentally shape how we see reality. If our glasses are tinted red and slightly unfocused we see a reddish, fuzzy world. We don't see reality as it is, we construct our reality as we perceive it through our invisible Core Beliefs, or our Big Assumptions. But there is hope here: "Surfacing Big Assumptions [and Inner Contradictions are] the royal road to seeing more deeply into ourselves and into the world we live in; to building greater capacity and complexity; to getting smarter, individually and organizationally."[24] (I would add that surfacing Big Assumptions are also the royal road to greater compassion, sustainability and spiritual simplicity . . . but that's for later).

Big Assumptions may be central to the individual lives we live and the world we build, but they are seldom discussed, because they are rarely seen. Herein lies the genius of Immunity to Change. We are not going to try to change our behaviors, or even our Competing Commitments. We are going to make our invisible Big Assumptions visible and gently entice them to grow up.

Moving to Column 4, Kegan and Lahey stress a couple of ways to access Big Assumptions. First, when our manager looks at her Column 3 Commitment; she asks, "What assumptions must I be making to have this Commitment?" The other approach is to look at the opposite of our Column 3 commitment. We ask our poor self-harassing manager to look at the opposite of her self-serving Commitment and complete a basic if/then statement: "I assume that if [I did the opposite] then . . ." Our manager's Commitment is to having everything perfect. So her sentence becomes, "I assume that if everything isn't perfect then I will look incompetent to my boss." And her self-dialogue might proceed like this:

Question: "And then?"

Response: "If I look incompetent to my boss I might be demoted."

Question: "And then?"

Response: "If I were demoted, I would be ashamed. People would see that I'm not

as capable as I pretend to be. My friends and colleagues would abandon me and I'd be all alone in the world. I might as well just die."

It sounds drastic, but the dire consequences are a good sign that she is getting to her Core Belief system. By their nature, Big Assumptions (Core Beliefs) reveal dire consequences in a hell we want to avoid. Even though they are not rational, they still run us. And you can see why they shape our actions so powerfully. If, like our manager, I believe that the consequence of incompetence is a profound loneliness and perhaps death, I'm going to make very sure that I never appear incompetent. I will have a compelling Commitment to perfectionism that guards against the horror of incompetence and will insure my survival by causing me to micromanage every project I oversee. Again, our manager's Column 2 behaviors are seen as inspired strategies for survival, given her Core Beliefs.

The good news is that, if our manager's Big Assumptions are the source of her *stuckness*, then they are also the means of her liberation. Having completed the four-column map of her Immunity to Change (see Figure 1.4), our manager is ready to move on to some deep, adaptive change.

COLUMN 1	COLUMN 2	COLUMN 3	COLUMN 4
NOBLE COMMITMENT (Improvement Goal)	DOING OR NOT DOING INSTEAD	COMPETING COMMITMENTS	BIG ASSUMPTIONS CORE BELIEFS
My goal is to delegate more effectively.	• Rather than wait, I just do the job on my own. • I get in the middle of everything and micromanage the process. • I over-explain.	***Worry Box*** They'll do it all wrong! - I'll look stupid! **Competing Commitments** • I am committed to having everything perfect. • I am committed to never looking stupid.	I assume that if everything isn't perfect then... • I'll look incompetent. • I'll be demoted. • I'll be ashamed. • I'll be abandoned • by friends and colleagues. • I'll be all alone. • I'll want to die.

Figure 1.4: Full Immunity to Change Map

WORKING WITH BIG ASSUMPTIONS

The obvious next question is, "Now that I have discovered a Big Assumption that invisibly runs my life, what can I do about it?" In Part Two I will develop a variety of tools available to small, caring groups but may not be workable in business, government and educational settings. For now, I will briefly mention the tools Kegan and Lahey use in these environments.

The four-column process opens a door that has probably been closed most of your life. There is a great opportunity here to make fundamental changes that can send your life on a different, more fulfilling trajectory. Kegan and Lahey offer a variety of strategies to challenge the veracity of Big Assumptions. The first is to just watch one of your Big Assumptions in action. Observe how it influences your day-to-day choices. Become deeply acquainted with when and how it is showing up and shaping what you do. Don't judge it, just notice it. (I call this *The Elephant's in Charge!*).

Once you have non-judgmentally watched your Big Assumption in action for a couple of weeks you can begin to test it (I call this *Check It Out!*). There are important criteria for choosing a test. Kegan and Lahey use the acronym SMART to summarize these criteria.

S: It's Safe. If your experiment to check out the validity of your Big Assumption goes wrong, the cost is inconsequential or at least negligible.

M: it's Modest. You are going to take baby steps. You are not trying to overthrow the Big Assumption all at once, but nudge it into greater maturity.

A: it's Actionable. You can actually run the experiment and do it soon.

R: it's Research. You are not looking to get rid of your Big Assumption or fundamentally change it. You're just getting information about it.

T: it's a Test. It's a little test that won't be complete until you bring back the results and explore the implications for your Big Assumption, and then design a next experiment.

This is just a brief introduction. A more thorough theoretical exploration can be found in Appendix A or in the superb texts by Kegan and Lahey. I will offer additional details as we explore and adapt this process for faith communities.

chapter 2
the faith setting

Faith is the bird that feels the light
when the dawn is still dark.
Rabindranath Tagore

This chapter is dedicated to the adventurous faith communities striving to lead the evolution of human consciousness for an emerging age. In the following pages I will outline the challenges and opportunities uniquely available to traditional faith communities that use Transformational Inquiry. I will then speak briefly to the new, emerging faith communities that are finding innovative ways to explore questions of ultimate concern.

IT'S ALL ABOUT ATTITUDE!

In working with various faith communities, I find it useful to frame our work as playfully as possible. The following is just one way to invite folks into that playfulness.

As humans, our most fervent desire is to get fixed! We all experience a sense of *lack* at the core of our being. We each have a hole at the deep center of our lives that we feel needs to be filled up. And, of course, we each believe we are the only one with that hole and so conclude *There is something wrong with me*. We spend our lives trying to fill that hole with something. . . anything. Our Big Assumptions and Core Beliefs are a couple of things we throw in there to fill up our lack. Since we all believes that *there is something wrong with me*, we all set about trying to get fixed. But it doesn't work! Trying to get fixed only confirms that we are unfixable. The problem is that the thing we are trying to fix is intrinsically unfixable. We are trying to take the *sense* of self that we believe is us, and make it a reality. But we can't make it real because it's not real; it is a construction of our minds. What we think of as *me* is nothing more than a swirl of self-confirming thoughts and emotions that create a sense of self. We call it ego. Ego is not bad. We need it to navigate in the material realm. It's just not real in the way we want it to be. We want it to have a special existence separate from, and exclusive of, all other things, especially other egos. But a part of us knows this is not possible. We know that we are fundamentally woven into this earth, into other beings, into the cosmos. If we look, we see our thoughts are constructed from the thoughts of others. We intuitively know that there is no separate *me* while we simultaneously believe there should be a separate *me*, otherwise, who am I? So, there must be something wrong with me and I need to get fixed! Aaaargh!

This is the human merry-go-round. It's the world of *samsara* (suffering) according to Buddhism. It's original sin according to Christianity. You may not be able to get off the merry-go-round, but you can loosen your grip. Buddhists inquire into the reality of the sense of self; Christians use love to unconditionally embrace the sense of self. Both, or either, allow you to fall through the constructed sense of self and find your true nature in the groundlessness of Eternity, in Joy.

Attitude is the key to returning to the Joy at the core of our being. A profound curiosity, grounded in the awareness that *I don't know* is the attitude that guides us through to the other side. From the Buddhist perspective it is *not knowing*, from the Christian orientation it is *self-emptying (kenosis)*, and from Islam it is *surrender*. In the Crazy Wisdom of Transformational Inquiry I ask you to assiduously pursue an attitude of curiosity. In other words, Don't Fix It! Don't advise, and don't counsel yourself or anyone else as we engage this work. Listen. Inquire. Open yourself to receive wisdom. If you like, make a game of it: On one side, assume that everyone you meet is an enlightened sage who has come to show you the way. Your job is to listen from your heart for the wisdom the universe is communicating to you through the person in front of you. On the other side, assume you are a wise person sent to help others discover their intrinsic divinity by listening deeply with love. In either case are you are not to fix or give advice because both will stifle the flow of wisdom and compassion.

CHALLENGES FOR TRADITIONAL FAITH COMMUNITIES

Established religious communities (what I refer to as traditional faith communities) offer a very different context than the business, government and educational settings where Immunity to Change has been so successfully applied. Kegan and Lahey's research emphasizes how essential a really strong Column 1 commitment is to the success of the change process. In the arenas of business, government and education, you typically have a group of individuals working together forty plus hours per week towards a common goal. These Individuals have a substantial personal investment in the success of the institution (or in doing their job well) if for no other reason than to retain employment. This kind of engagement is ideal for motivating change.

Traditional faith communities are quite different. They are primarily volunteer organizations with diffuse (often abstract) goals and intermittent involvement—the opposite of the motivation in other institutions. It is challenging for those in faith communities to find the clear, action-oriented Noble Commitments so essential for Kegan and Lahey's work. As a result, it is often very difficult for them to consistently test their Big Assumptions, even when they want to change. The dramatically different context of traditional religious communities brings both challenges and opportunities. First, a look at the challenges.

While Transformational Inquiry can be an important developmental tool for leaders of traditional faith communities, its real potential lies in engaging members throughout the community. The staff of institutional faith communities is paid to be there: members are not. Rather, members are asked to pay to support the community. Members are not employees whose performance will influence their job tenures. They may act like *employees* when they volunteer; like *customers* when they receive the various services offered by the community; and as *employers* when in leadership positions. The staff is literally employed by the members, but members often don't have the deeply-felt ownership and empowerment felt by business employers, managers or even public sector employers.

In guiding congregants through Inquiry, it is important to remember the different motivations of the participants. Congregants don't need to undertake practices they may perceive as threatening, challenging or scary. There are no mandates that individuals must explore their inner depths because they are part of a congregation. The articulation of the faith may recommend it, and there may be significant social pressure, but individuals are not required to change to maintain their membership. In fact, there is a systemic motivation to *not* push people too hard lest they withdraw their financial, emotional and personal support. The notion that the pastor's role is to "comfort the afflicted and afflict the comfortable" often retreats during these days of declining faith to "comforting the afflicted and reassuring the comfortable." So, while folks may want to make personal changes, especially during times of crisis, there is really nothing holding their toes to the fire. As a member of a faith community, I can dabble in personal transformation, but unless I'm really hurting, there is no requirement to take it very seriously. And even if I am in crisis, I may engage only long enough to alleviate the immediate pain, but not long enough to take on the more prolonged process of personal transformation.

Hence, the first challenge facing a facilitator of Transformational Inquiry in a faith setting is a generally tepid commitment to change. This shows up as early as the Column 1 Noble Commitment. In contrast, the work setting is generally full of very concrete improvement goals, like our example in the previous chapter: *I want to delegate better*. In the faith community I often hear more general goals, like *I'd like to be more peaceful*, or *I'd like to deepen my prayer life*, or *I'd like to be less anxious*. These less specific commitments, or goals, can be very fruitful. They hold great potential for the deep, personal transformation in the traditional faith setting. The challenge is to articulate these less specific goals in ways that can lead individuals into greater depths of discovery. In the next chapter, I will explore some useful techniques for getting to a powerful Column 1 Commitment.

The second challenge also stems from the volunteer nature of faith communities. That challenge is to maintain the energy required to work on Big Assumptions in the absence of financial motivation and regular contact. Most of us have spent twenty, thirty, forty years or more defending ourselves against seeing our Competing Commitments and Big Assumptions. In a business setting, livelihood is a potent motivator for change. This motivator is, of course, absent in volunteer faith communities. In more than a decade of leading Transformational Inquiry in my church, I find that folks balk at the demands of the iterative Safe Tests employed by Kegan and Lahey. That's why I have developed a variety of strategies to keep folks engaged longer (see chapter 4).

No doubt, traditional faith communities present formidable challenges to deep developmental work. Yet I believe, the possibility for profound personal change in a faith setting far exceeds the challenges and even outstrips the opportunities available in business, government or education.

OPPORTUNITIES FOR TRADITIONAL FAITH COMMUNITIES

Institutional religious communities appear to have three tasks and some unique characteristics that make Transformational Inquiry a very powerful tool. The three tasks are:

1. helping individuals develop a deeper awareness of, or closer relationship to, the Divine (spirituality),
2. building a community of caring, love and support, and
3. furthering an understanding of justice in the world.

Here, I want to dive more deeply into the unique opportunities faith communities, as institutions, bring to our world.

Developing a deeper awareness of the Divine, building a caring community, and practicing justice all require increased awareness of the factors that *prevent* their realization. Legal, political, and economic institutions can impede each of these goals. Even though faith communities often have little direct influence over these institutions it doesn't mean they can't exert influence. Their influence comes from their power over the cultural stories that define the values and the personal meaning-making stories we each construct to guide our lives. In a democratic society, we hope that our economic and political structures will reflect our most deeply held values. This is where faith communities play a pivotal role.

As meaning-making creatures, each of us lives from a personal story that in some way answers the questions: Who am I? Why am I here? What is my purpose? How will I know if I've realized my purpose? Where am I going? What happens when I die? . . . and more. These questions, and myriad answers, spin around in our minds like a great whirlpool with many self-reinforcing currents and eddies. We call the sum total of these currents and eddies *identity* or *ego*. When we think of ourselves, we typically refer to those interlocking stories, beliefs, emotions and experiences that declare *this is me!* The Story of Me does not arise spontaneously within each of us. The raw material for the Story of Me comes from the culture in which we are imbedded. We draw on the stories and explanations, the beliefs and emotions, and the experiences and doubts presented by the culture we're born into. As Ortega y Gasset says "Life is fired at us point blank." We have no choice but to construct ourselves from the material presented to us by our culture. As children we lack the power to discriminate which beliefs or stories will serve us, so we absorb them uncritically. Many are pre-verbal. They may have served us well when we were children but they probably don't serve us well as adults. Adulthood invariably requires more nuanced stories, stories that incorporate subtle changes to the foundational story.

Cultural stories and personal meaning-making have long been the province of faith communities. Even though Christian churches in the West have been slow to keep up with the times, they still possess a vast trove of cultural stories that weave deeply through our psyches. These stories are often invisible to us. But they are there. In a previous book, *Reverent Irreverence,* I told the story of racing to the hospital, fearful that I was having a heart attack (I wasn't). As my wife drove me down a mountain, I wondered, *If I die would I go to hell?* I concluded that a merciful God would never let anyone go to hell. As comforting as that conclusion was, it wasn't the point. The point was that I wasn't a Christian, my parents hadn't been Christians, and I'd little connection with church in my life; but there it was—the Christian story alive and well in a heathen.

As I mentioned in the Introduction, churches and other faith communities *own* the great cultural mythologies that provide the content for our personal meaning-making stories. As such, faith communities have both the opportunity and the obligation to adapt their stories to meet the needs of the times. This doesn't mean they must change their values or commitments whenever popular opinion changes. But they do need to reframe of their traditions to meet arising needs. Transformational Inquiry can be a tool for examining the beliefs that we receive from our faith traditions and questioning them. Faith communities, especially traditional religious communities that encourage broad interpretation of their belief systems, create a potentially transforming environment wherein individuals receive permission to alter their Core Beliefs. I don't know of another institution that has such potential to support fundamental change.

In addition to possessing the stories that put our lives in context, faith communities also have society's permission to transform individuals to their core. Whereas psychology has permission to *fix* people, faiths are invited to *remake* people. Where psychology builds strong egos, faiths can take folks entirely beyond their egos. Business and government leaders who explore Immunity to Change on a personal level can make adaptive changes in their ego structures that will help them work more effectively. Transformational Inquiry in the faith setting fundamentally challenges the dominance of the ego and lets the Divine shine through. Again, I know of no other institutional setting that can so fully nurture this possibility.

Finally, faith communities possess one of our society's scarcest resources: *time.* In a world driven by profit and achievement and addicted to every distraction, it is very hard to find time, not just for reflection, but for hanging out with whatever changes might be going through us. We might say that faith communities have *God's time.* In that sense, faith communities are *outside of time*. This is so countercultural that it is difficult to find language for it. The job of faith communities is to engage the Infinite, which means that instead of trying to get things done *on time*, our job is to support individuals as the Great Mystery unfolds through them. You might say this is the Crazy Wisdom at the core of every religion.

Practically speaking, faith communities don't have to produce outcomes to satisfy a corporate or governmental board; their job is to *allow*, listen to and nurture what is unfolding. Since our culture, our society, and our stress-driven selves seem largely incapable of such allowing, faith communities can offer a socially legitimate space to engage a different kind of time. Transformational Inquiry becomes a tool for holding the paradoxes of our humanness unsolved so that Crazy Wisdom can *solve us*. No other institution has been given this license by society.

EMERGING FAITH COMMUNITIES

As we often hear, traditional faith communities are on the decline. Often, they are replaced by small, intimate groups . . . *home churches*. While these new communities lack the authority to change the great mythic stories of our culture, they often have the derived authority to change people at their core and to take the time required to help individuals make deep change. These alternative, emerging faith communities offer an ideal setting for the Crazy Wisdom tools of Transformational Inquiry. Individuals drawn to such communities are often motivated to make the kind of personal changes required for spiritual development. The tools in this book will serve you well in your search for deep spiritual transformation.

chapter 3

a multitude
of cosmologies

*Do I contradict myself? Very well, then I contradict
myself, I am large, I contain multitudes.*
Walt Whitman

A core premise of Transformational Inquiry is that we must, and
actually do, create our own theologies from which we construct lives that
are meaningful to us. Since birth, culture greets us point-blank, we have no
choice but to absorb the meaning-making structure into which we are born.
And this meaning-making structure of our culture is always implicated in
Big Assumptions that guide our lives invisibly. Challenging or questioning
into the Big Assumptions that guide our lives entails a risk to our core
identity. Challenging a personal Big Assumption implies challenging the
larger meaning-making structure of our culture.

As Kegan consistently points out, personal evolution requires a
context that is judiciously balanced between challenge and support.
When we challenge the Big Assumptions that are derived from the larger
cultural context that gives our lives meaning, we must have escape routes.
If challenging our Big Assumptions implicitly challenges the story of our
culture, we need a quiver full of metaphors that allow us to reinterpret
our culture's message without destroying the fundamental cohesion it
brings to both our individual and interpersonal lives. In the following
sections I offer a grab bag of metaphors and philosophical perspectives
that can be adapted to our own personal needs as we engage the process
of Transformational Inquiry.

I begin with a humble apology. I am about to adulterate several of the world's great stories, both secular and sacred. In the following pages, I will offer a spectrum of grossly oversimplified theories on the *nature of the universe* (cosmologies) and undoubtedly misrepresent all of them to a greater or lesser degree. Fortunately, my goal is not philosophical or theological purity, it is practicality. And practicality invites me into the presumptuous position of trying to say something meaningful about a variety of cosmologies I only marginally understand. I do this because they represent a meaningful portion of the contemporary Western milieu.

We have become a multi-faith culture. We moderns have access to the world's wisdom traditions, sacred and secular, with little or none of the discipline or culture that gave them their formative depth. We glibly mix and match cosmologies in the natural ebb and flow of our lives. I doubt that we would find a pure Buddhist, Christian or atheist in the Western world. We are *all* multi-faith to some degree or another. This multi-faith culture is the appropriate context for our work in Transformational Inquiry.

I offer this smorgasbord of cosmologies for two reasons: first, to provide a variety of legitimate cosmologies individuals can draw from as they question into the fundamental structures of their own personal meaning-making stories; and, second, to give individuals permission to creatively rework their personal meaning-making stories as well as their culture's great mythological story. In my work with Transformational Inquiry, it has proved important to answer "Yes!" to everyone's exploration. Every individual courageous enough to step in and challenge a Big Assumption deserves to know that the reconstruction that works for them is welcome.

The danger, of course, is that our work can degenerate into an incoherent mess of mixed-up cosmologies. This is a real danger that emerges if the focus of this work is confined strictly to the intellect. The practice of *faith* helps guard against a postmodern relativism taking over the process. I don't mean faith as some kind of belief system, but faith as a felt sense of abiding in something greater. In Christian language, this felt sense comes with *kenosis*, self-emptying. In more contemporary spiritual language, it's called *presence*. In practice, it is about listening deeply to the truth that our bodies, our feelings, our intuitions, and *something more* that is revealed at all points in this process.

A second strategy I use to avoid the relativistic trap is to emphasize the developmental evolution of the individual. Transformational Inquiry claims there is a hierarchical sequence that individuals move through in their development, and that each step unmasks a hidden Big Assumption. Every time people unearth a hidden Big Assumption, their perspectives become more encompassing and their capacity for caring deepens.

In my experience, the Big Assumptions that undermine our most noble aspirations are universally grounded in fear. Any lessening of our attachment to a Big Assumption correspondingly reduces our fear. When we are less fearful, we are more willing to embrace expansive ideas and emotions. The developmental orientation of Transformational Inquiryprovides a structure that permits us to view the different metaphors offered in this section as tools for the unfolding of our hearts and minds into greater awareness and caring.

In keeping with this intention, I will draw on the cosmologies presented in this section and use them as sacred reference points for different tools of Transformational Inquiry in the following chapters. My purpose is to suggest how each step of the Transformational Inquiry process is connected to a larger, nurturing cosmology. The point is to remind us at every step of the way that we are engaged in a sacred activity of immense importance to a Mystery we can never define.

Cosmology I:
The World is Made of Stories

The universe is made of stories, not atoms.
Muriel Rukeyser

Not atoms? Of course it is made of atoms, that's one of
our important stories.
David Loy

The world we live in is made of stories. Within those larger stories are little stories that run around in our heads and tell us who we are. Mind-chatter says things like: "That shouldn't have happened." "I like him." "She's driving too fast." and "I hope it doesn't rain." Then there are the bigger stories, stories around which we build a sense of self: "I'm too fat." "I'm really a nice person." "Most people just aren't as smart as me." and "People don't really like me." Then there are the really, really big stories we called Myths. These are the stories that orchestrate our culture and tell us who we are in the universe. Myths provide the cultural context in which we construct our own personal stories. We have these stories in our head, but they get real traction when we share them with other people. The people who share and affirm our stories we call friends; the ones who challenge our stories we call enemies.

Our stories are vital to us because the narratives swirling in our minds create the sense of *me*. It's been said that we have over 70,000 thoughts a day; not different thoughts, but a small number that are repeated over and over again. These thoughts define who we are moment by moment. When our thoughts stop, our sense of self stops. If thoughts stop for too long, we get scared. When I am not constructing my sense of self there is the fear that I will disappear. The fear of annihilation that arises if I spend too much time *not* constructing myself keeps me thinking compulsively, making internal comments that assure that my sense of self will continue. This appears fundamental to the nature of human beings. We cannot *not* create a sense of self. However, we can, as the spiritual traditions teach us, not take that construction too seriously. We can step back from that constructed sense of self, gain perspective, and reshape the story in our minds.

In a very real sense, the story I construct in my mind, which is largely the story I receive from my culture, my family and my peers, tells me who I am. If that were the full story, there would be no hope of changing anything. I would be fully determined. But that is not the case. We all have the capacity to step outside of our stories. We do this in stages. As we mature we can take on or expand perspectives which will deliver different insights into the personas we are constructing in our daily chatter. The psychospiritual project, according to this cosmology, is to construct increasingly expansive understandings of ourselves until, with awakening, we can inhabit a *God's-eye view* of who we are.

On a larger stage, our families, our communities, our cities, states, and nations, are constructed through the stories we collectively nurture and cultivate. When the world is constructed from our stories, changing our personal stories becomes a path to changing our world. The work we do in Transformational Inquiry helps us to find and create more expansive perspectives from which to engage the story of *me*, my family, my community, etc.

Because each of us lives in a world constructed from stories, there is a dark cloud of annihilation hovering over each and every one of us that drives us. This cloud is, according to David Loy, the sense of *lack* we all feel because our constructed sense of self is illusory. According to Loy's Buddhist orientation, we each experience a profound sense of lack because deep down we know the sense of self we create is an illusion, created by thoughts swirling in our heads, thoughts affirmed and confirmed by our emotions. This is not just a Buddhist insight; the Christian notion of original sin points to the same experience. It is the sense that *there is something wrong with me*. Christians claim we inherited it from Adam and Eve, fundamentalists say we have a *God-sized hole* at our center. Both point to this sense of lack. The project of the illusory sense of self, the ego, is to deny, bury, or destroy, if possible, this sense of lack. Our entire society is oriented toward eliminating this sense of lack. The problem is, our sense of lack cannot be eliminated or filled up by anything we do. The spiritual traditions agree that the only way out of our sense of lack is to walk right into it. The Buddha chose to sit under the Bodhi tree and either awaken or die; Jesus acquiesced to crucifixion. Both of them walked boldly into the utter terror at the core of their being; and confronted the cloud of annihilation hovering over all of us.

If the world is made of stories, if my individual sense of self, my community, my culture, and the world I live in are all constructed of such stories, each one intended to reduce the darkness of the cloud of annihilation that hovers over me, what am I to do? Transformational Inquiry is a process which, in the wise hands of the faith community, can walk us into our sense of lack, enable us to directly confront our fear of annihilation, and recognize the profound grace at the core of our fear.

COSMOLOGY II: SOPHIA PERENNIS

My presentation of *Sofia Perennis* (perennial wisdom), comes from the work of Lynn Baumann. The story I tell falls far short of the deep wisdom revealed in his articulation of Sofia Perennis. Nonetheless, he has graciously allowed me to use the graphic presentation below to summarize this expansive myth. It is important to remember that a myth, by its nature, is non-rational, or more precisely, trans-rational (beyond rational). Though slightly different from my presentation of Sofia Perennis, Aldous Huxley's summary of the perennial philosophy is instructive. He describes the perennial philosophy as: "the thing—the metaphysic that recognizes a divine Reality substantial to the world of things and lives and minds; the psychology that finds in the soul something similar to, or even identical with, divine Reality; the ethic that places man's final end in the knowledge of the immanent and transcendent Ground of all being—the thing is immemorial

and universal." As Baumann suggests, Sofia Perennis "nucleates" the world's religions, it is the meta-story around which the world's faith systems are built. We begin this story at the top of the graphic with the facial profile. This is, in Huxley's terms, "the divine Reality substantial to the world of things and lives in minds." It is the Great Mystery, the Godhead, spaciousness, the great emptiness which contains all, etc. It is depicted with a profile to indicate its reality. Even though it is beyond all speaking, it is real. Even though it cannot be conceptualized, it is the foundation of all concepts. In the language of Taoism, it is the Tao that cannot be spoken.

This divine reality manifests itself first within a walled garden. We are nurtured there by the divine feminine, Sofia, the queen of heaven. Sofia is the mother of all creation. This walled garden, in Abrahamic faiths, is Eden. We abide in Eden, outside of space and time, until it is time for us to develop. We abide there as our essential selves, an integral component of the inseparable whole called Humanity. We come into creation at our choosing. Our willingness to manifest in space and time makes us heroes in the eyes of the Divine. The earth, Flatland, is created as a stage for our journey. In our journey across Flatland (the parallelogram at the bottom of the graphic), we discover who we truly are.

All meaning is created in the dual world of space and time, the material world of Flatland. We began with a world of possibilities contained within us, like the acorn that will become a mighty oak. Though life greets us point-blank, we are not without resources. We are supported by all the faith traditions, here represented by Moses (on the lower left).

We are part of the caravan across linear time. The Star of David at the bottom of the graphic represents a map suggested by the second chapter of the Gospel of Thomas: "Yeshua says, 'If you are *searching*, you must not stop until you *find*. When you find, however, you will become *troubled*. Your confusion will give way to *wonder*. In wonder you will *reign* over all things. Your sovereignty will be your *rest*.'" It is analogous to the roadmap of the Christian liturgical year which begins with Advent, then continues with Christmas, Epiphany, Lent, Easter and Pentecost. (I present both of these maps below.)

As we progress across Flatland we collect stories of our journey. The stories are of two types: the stories that twist and twine through our minds to create our illusory sense of self, and the stories inspired by the Divine, here represented by the bee pollinating the flower. As we become increasingly adept at differentiating between these stories, we grow and mature, our souls deepen. This is comparable to Huxley's notion of "the psychology that finds in the soul something similar to, or even identical with, divine Reality."

The complex symbol in the lower right area of the graphic expresses our growing maturity. The rose surrounded by a heart at the root of the picture depicts our compassionate core in Sofia. The tree is our maturing self. And the blue angel (our soul) is the analog of the icon of our true selves, the Angel above. The Angel is our essential nature, experienced as a guardian angel which guides us through Flatland. It is constantly in communication with our souls to create fully-formed images as represented by the tree. The fullness of our life on earth is comprised of the sacred stories of our journeys through Flatland. Our personal stories become aspects of the holographic Human, the Anthropos (center of the graphic), which, in turn, is watched over by the Divine Mother, Sofia. In Huxley's language, this is the ethic that finds our identity in the Divine.

As an individual, I become my true self when I put myself fully into the story and connect to the whole body of humanity. The process intensifies my being by drawing down the qualities of heaven and embodying them. Hence the Christian quote: "Your will be done on earth as it is in heaven."

In sum, each of us is a mirror- image of God projected into space and time. We need God because we are the divine story being told in space and time. God needs us because we are God's way of making order out of chaos. Our stories are "the record of the opening of an inner world that reveals the transcendent individuality of the human person." Our desire to return home to our true nature is experienced as a deep longing that is an integral part of us.

COSMOLOGY III: THE NEW SCIENCE

The new story of science emerges from the understanding of our universe that has developed over the past century. Particularly in the past half-century, science has discovered a universe more vast than we could have imagined. Not only are we *not* the center of the universe, as Copernicus pointed out five centuries ago, we are just one planet, circling one star, at the edge of a galaxy containing two or three hundred billion stars, in a universe of hundreds of billions of galaxies. Not only that, this universe has been expanding for nearly 14 billion years, and continues to expand, at an increasing rate. This new understanding of the universe has created something of an existential crisis. Who are we then? How do we fit? Where are we going? How can my life be meaningful?

A new story is emerging in both a macro and micro perspective. The macro perspective I offer comes from theoretical physicist Brian Swimme. In Swimme's story, the universe is not aimless or random, nor is it simply a place or mechanism. It is a sacred event that has been unfolding for nearly

14 billion years. It is an unfolding of great beauty and depth that appears to be developing with a slant towards life and intelligence in a very complex manner. The tendency toward life shows up in profound moments of grace. According to Swimme,

> Photosynthesis is one such moment of grace. About 3.9 billion years ago, the planet faced a crisis when the early Earth's generation of chemically-rich compounds was slowing just at a time when the population of prokaryotic cells (bacteria and blue-green algae, for example) feeding off the compounds was expanding exponentially. Instead of a major die-off from starvation, some prokaryotes learned to capture photons hurtling at the speed of light from the sun and convert them into food. The result, photosynthesis, was a creative act of elegance born out of crisis.

When plants learned to capture energy from the sun, all higher life forms became possible.

Humans represent another moment of grace. We are a species capable of reflecting upon the universe and our role in it. As such, we can consciously choose the kind of world we want to make. As Swimme says, "The universe is permeated by cosmological powers that wove us into being, and we are those powers in a new form."

This new cosmology offers an elegant answer to the pressing existential questions of Who are we? How do we fit? Where are we going? How can my life be meaningful? The answer is, we are consciously self-aware, spiritual participants at the leading edge of evolution.

Taking the micro view, quantum physicist Amit Goswami validates much of Swimme's story, but from the perspective of the tiny. He and Swimme agree that material science does not present the whole picture. According to Goswami,

> Materialist science takes it as its basic axiom that everything is matter. We have literally managed to train a whole generation of students on the idea that everything is material, but this Newtonian world view that has shaped our understanding for centuries is now giving way to the revelations of quantum physics which goes beyond materialism; to show that consciousness, not matter, is the ground of all being.

You can call this consciousness God, if you like, or you can call it quantum consciousness if you prefer. As Goswami expresses it, God has three distinct characteristics that derive from quantum physics: *nonlocality, discontinuity,* and *tangled hierarchy.*

Nonlocality points to the discovery that interactions are possible outside of space and time. In contrast to the assumptions of material science, individuals can interrelate with one another instantaneously in the quantum realm. In nonlocal communication, we transcend the local ego mind and momentarily engage quantum consciousness. In other words, in the silence between thoughts we access a vast multitude of possibilities from which consciousness can select.

Discontinuity offers another access point to divine consciousness. "In quantum physics, objects are not determined things—they are quantum possibilities for consciousness to choose from. When an observer looks, the possibility wave changes into actuality. Colloquially we say, the wave collapses into a particle, a quantum event." Another way of saying this is that when an observer looks at a possibility it becomes a reality. But "there is no mathematics for collapse; no continuous algorithm can be given for it. Collapse is discontinuous." According to Goswami, discontinuity can be accessed in conversation with others when we listen without judgment and pay attention with respect. "In quantum dialoguing, you also include speaking from the silence to give non-locality a chance to work its magic." We experience this as intuition. "Intuition is your glimpse at a future quantum leap." Just remember, your "intention for manifestation must resonate with nonlocal consciousness" or it will fail. In other words, your desires must resonate with Infinite Consciousness.

Quantum measurement in the brain is called *tangled hierarchy.* This simply means that there is a circular relationship among the components of the brain. A tangled hierarchy occurs when you move up or down through a hierarchical system, then find yourself back where you started. Consider the paradoxical nature of the sentence "I am a liar." If I am truly a liar and I say to you 'I am a liar,' then I'm telling you the truth. But if I'm telling you the truth, then I am not a liar. The loop continues indefinitely. This, of course, is a conundrum within the arbitrary rules of grammar. But in the brain, tangled hierarchy is compulsory. It is one of the laws of the universe that brings about manifest experience. According to Goswami, ego establishes a simple hierarchical relationship with the world.

> To regain the tangled hierarchy of the quantum self-experience, we use intimate relationships in which conflicts arise . . . Unresolved conflicts generate new possibilities for consciousness to process, but only quantum consciousness–God–can process the new. When a new creative insight

comes from this kind of processing, often the insight is also the discovery of the 'otherness' of the other. From this discovery, we can love 'other' unconditionally . . .

A lovely example of tangled hierarchy in the Christian tradition is the commandment to love your neighbor as yourself.

In the emerging story of the new cosmology, we are children of stardust, stardust that is intrinsically conscious. We are an integral part of the 14-billion-year evolution of our universe. As self-aware spiritual beings, we humans have an essential role to play in the unfolding of the universe. Our choices matter. It is essential that we attend to the source and implications of those choices. Will we choose according to our self-serving egos, or will we seek a deeper source? While we would all like to make choices that improve our individual lives, our capacity to influence Infinite Consciousness is miniscule. In other words, there is free will, but personal will is tiny.

As Goswami states, "The sum and substance of conditioning is that as consciousness progressively identifies with the ego, there is a corresponding loss of freedom." Fortunately, we never close down completely. Even in the conditioning of our egos, we retain some freedom, at least the freedom to occasionally say *no* to our conditioning. Herein lies the hope of what Goswami calls *quantum activism*: use of our limited freedom to access the quantum tools of nonlocality, discontinuity, and tangled hierarchy to open ourselves to quantum consciousness, or God, and fulfill our proper role in the universe.

COSMOLOGY IV: NEUROPSYCHOLOGY— REWIRING THE MATERIAL BRAIN

In contrast to the expansive New Science represented by Swimme and Goswami, neuroscience, and its subfield, neuropsychology, are grounded in a strict materialism that says emphatically that there is only matter: all of reality is apprised of particles and energies shaped by material forces. There is no spirit, no "spooky action at a distance," nothing beyond the astonishingly complex interaction of material components. This materialism is the foundation of The Modern Story expressed in chapter 1. Within the materialist cosmology, neuroscience is becoming an increasingly important explanatory story for Western culture. We could borrow from many different examples for reference points. But, for simplicity, I will share a particularly poignant example: the application of neuropsychology to a problem of brain misfiring.

Jeffrey Schwartz is a neuropsychologist at UCLA. His patients suffer from obsessive compulsive disorder, or OCD. For example, some patients obsessively wash their hands, and others repeat a particular phrase over and over again. Schwartz has had remarkable success helping them using four steps reflective of Transformational Inquiry. An extraordinary outcome of his work is that by helping folks to gain perspective on their OCD, Schwartz is able to show changes in the electrical firing of their brains. In other words, his patients are literally *rewiring their brains*.

Bringing a background of mindfulness practice to his work, Schwartz first has his patients *relabel* their compulsion by teaching them to recognize an OCD-related thought as soon as possible and to relabel it as *unreal*. As one patient responded, "It's not me! It's my OCD!"

His second strategy emerged from his frustration with stubborn symptoms. In one session a patient asked him "Doc, can you just tell me why the damn thing keeps bothering me—why it doesn't go away?" Schwartz happened to be carrying around some brain scans of OCD patients. "You want to know why it doesn't go away?" Schwartz said. "I'll show you why." He grabbed the scan he had been working with and pointed to a section of the brain and said, "Look here, your brain is absurdly overactive." His patients' response was immediate, their faces changed and the excitement was palpable: Their strange thoughts and compulsive behaviors were no longer *theirs*; they were just faulty transmissions of a malfunctioning brain. Hence, his second step: *reattribute*. Schwartz taught his patients to reattribute their OCD symptoms to their gnarled brain wiring, and thereby meaningfully separate it from their sense of self.

His third tactic was to help clients focus on something besides the intrusive OCD thoughts. Recalling his meditation practice of returning attention to the breath when distracted, Schwartz gave his patients permission to turn their attention to a healthy behavior to distract them from their OCD behavior. He called this *refocusing*.

Schwartz's culminating step is *revaluing*. The OCD thoughts that patients once considered so important were to be systematically deconstructed, understood and finally revalued as, in Schwartz's words, " . . . trash . . . Not worth the gray matter they rode in on." Conversely, Schwartz's patients learned to value their non-OCD behaviors highly.

COSMOLOGY V: THE LAW OF THREE

This cosmological metaphor comes from the mystical insights of the mysterious dancing master of Central Asia, Gurdjieff. My oversimplified explanation is derived from the work of contemporary mystic Cynthia

Bourgeault. In her compelling treatise, *The Holy Trinity and the Law of Three: Discovering the Radical Truth at the Heart of Christianity,* Bourgeault develops an evolutionary understanding of the Christian Trinity with important implications for our work in Transformational Inquiry. Again, my purpose is to offer yet another metaphor upon which you can draw to place the seemingly mundane work of Transformational Inquiry in a spiritual context. With the Law of Three, I invite you to notice how our work with Transformational Inquiry engages a fundamental evolutionary process of the universe.

Bourgeault argues that "The Trinity is primarily about how God moves and flows, how God changes from one form (or 'state') into another within the domain of manifestation, and in turn penetrates the mutability of creation with the wholeness of divine being."

We in the West are acculturated into either/or thinking. We tend to think that truth lies with one side or another. According to Bourgeault, in such a binary system, "life sustains and expresses itself in the tension of opposites, and a slackening of this tension through an imbalance of the parts leads to a collapse of the whole system." In contrast, in a ternary, or three-part system, two polarities call forth a third, or *reconciling* principle. "In contrast to a binary system, which finds stability in the balance of opposites, the ternary system stipulates a third force that emerges as the necessary mediation of these opposites and that in turn . . . generates a synthesis at a whole new level. It is a dialectic whose resolution simultaneously creates a new realm of possibility."

While a binary system suggests cyclical recurrence, the asymmetry of the Law of Three indicates a dynamic process of evolution. The Law of Three stipulates that all phenomena spring from the interaction of three forces: the first *active,* the second *passive*, and the third, *neutralizing*. It is important to realize that the third force, neutralizing, is an independent force, coequal with the other two. It is not a product of the first two as in the classic Hegelian "thesis, antithesis, synthesis." Rather, the third force brings the other two forces into relationship and creates something new. "Just as it takes three independent strands of hair to make a braid, so it takes three individual lines of force to make a new arising."

The Law of Three emphasizes that all three forces are equally important. For example, the second force, denying, is an essential component of a new arising. "The '*enemy*' is never the enemy but a necessary part of the 'givens' in any situation, and solutions will never work that have as their goal the elimination of the second force." Imagine, reflects Bourgeault, "how greatly the political and religious culture wars of our era could be eased by this simple courtesy of the Law of Three: (1) the enemy is never the problem but the opportunity; (2) the problem will never be solved through eliminating or silencing the opposition but only through (3) creating a new field of possibility large enough to hold the tension of opposites and launch them in a new direction."

As we will discover as we dive more deeply into the Crazy Wisdom tools Transformational Inquiry, our commitment to exploration, to an openhearted inquiry into the source of our suffering is intrinsically a third force activity.

COSMOLOGY VI: CHRISTIAN JOURNEYS OF AWAKENING

This section briefly presents two maps of spiritual awakening from the Christian tradition. The first, hidden in plain sight, is the liturgical year. It runs from Advent to Christmas, through Epiphany, on to Lent and Holy week, then to Easter and finally to Pentecost. It is said to replicate the life of Jesus. The second map comes from a different track of Christianity, not included in its canon, the Gospel of Thomas.

Map 1: The Liturgical Year

The Christian liturgical year begins with Advent which represents the dawning of awareness. It is the first glimmer that things are not as we thought. It offers the merest taste and is likely to slip away for days or even years; but once you have glimpsed awareness you must eventually seek.

Christmas is the breakthrough comprehension, symbolized in the birth of Jesus that begins to change everything. It is as if we are seeing for the first time. It can be as small as some concept we have been trying to wrap our minds around and suddenly understand; or as grand as a mystical vision that fundamentally shifts our perception of reality. In the process of personal awakening, the glimpse offered by Advent may motivate you to turn your attention inward. Christmas is your reward for beginning that inward journey.

The fundamental shift in perception born at Christmas begins to reveal a whole new world of insights, symbolized by the season of Epiphany. As we begin to see with new eyes and a new mind, great treasures unfold before us. This can be an ecstatic journey as we explore the implications of our new awareness.

It is, perhaps, our greatest hope that Epiphany will last forever, but Lent is just around the corner. Eternal Epiphany is the principal promise of today's spiritual marketplace. Yet, it is still an early movement of spiritual awakening. Advent, Christmas and Epiphany have an additive flavor as more insights are added to our understanding as we progress through these celebrations. But spiritual awakening, salvation, requires *subtraction*. Lent begins the process of subtraction. The positive, wonderful revelations of Epiphany confirm our sense of self, the building up of identity; but salvation requires the stripping away of the self. In Lent, we journey into the shadows . . . the hell we have avoided. In Lent, we challenge everything we thought was true.

The fundamental insight of Lent is that, yes, there is light at the end of the tunnel, but it's an oncoming train. Passion, or Holy Week, symbolizes the final destruction of the ego, our illusory sense of a separate self. God does not want *most* of us; God wants *all* of us, stripped naked and simple. At the culmination of Lent we must walk, or be pushed, in front of the train.

The incredible discovery of Easter is that what we most feared does not come to pass. The I, the ego I always thought I was, has died, yet I exist, but not as I thought I did (language is not our friend here!). Not only is there an I that exists, but it inhabits a realm of freedom, of spaciousness, never imagined as possible. Easter represents the full awakening of the Christ within.

We're not done yet. The all-important season of Pentecost is about integrating the transformations from Advent through Easter. In the symbolism of the Liturgical Year, we are now on our own. Each of us must integrate the changes we have been through. Salvation, resurrection, enlightenment mean nothing until they are brought back into everyday life, and that is the task of Pentecost. No surprise, it is the longest season of the Liturgical Year.

Map 2: The Gospel of Thomas

The Gospel of Thomas was discovered near Nag Hammadi, Egypt in 1945. It is a sayings gospel with no narrative story. Scholars estimate its date as early as 40 A.D., others as late as 140 A.D. Bible scholar, Lynn Baumann, argues that Logian 2 offers a map of the spiritual journey:

Yeshua says . . .

> If you are *searching*, you must not stop until you *find*.
> When you find, however, you will become *troubled*.
> Your confusion will give way to *wonder*.
> In wonder you will *reign* over all things.
> Your sovereignty will be your *rest*.

Using the Star of David, Baumann creates a map of the spiritual journey based on this saying.

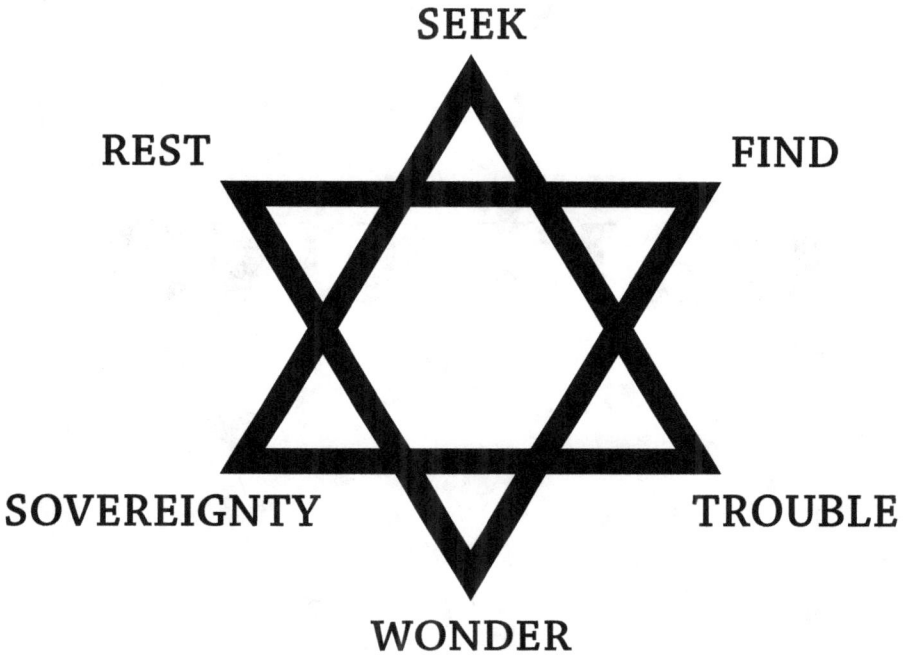

SEEK

REST

FIND

SOVEREIGNTY

TROUBLE

WONDER

This appears to be a very simple map with many similarities to the liturgical year. We will keep it simple for our purposes. It says simply, seek and you will find, and when you find you will be troubled. If you embrace your trouble and confusion, your confusion will give way to wonder. As you live this wonder, you will become a master of a new form of consciousness and find abiding rest. The Gospel of Thomas appears to be an elaboration of a simple map.

part two

the crazy wisdom tools of transformational inquiry

chapter 4
first steps

If the world is crying out for a new order of consciousness, that is, a new way of knowing, being, and caring, the question is, *How*? The problem is that rational, linear thought won't get us there. Reason will do a lot of wonderful things but, as Einstein quipped, "you can't solve your problems with the consciousness that created them." We in the modern world are in just such a position. The emergence of reason and rationality in the West during the Enlightenment brought us many blessings; yet the curses, which always come with a vast new way of knowing, are only now being fully felt. Rationality has brought us riches, opportunities, and benefits beyond our wildest expectations, but it has also created existential threats to humanity. We cannot simply will ourselves to do things differently. We need access to deeper sources of wisdom.

But deep wisdom is seldom granted to logic. Because the means by which we access deep wisdom are so counter to conventional thought, they are perceived as crazy. Yet it is precisely the crazy, paradoxical nature of these tools that opens the door to different ways of knowing and being. Wherever you are on a journey of awakening consciousness, the next step is always mysterious, confusing, and frightening. The tools, collectively called Transformational Inquiry, are precisely the paradoxical tools of Crazy Wisdom. Again, Crazy Wisdom tells us that

Judgments reveal nobility.
Blame inspires hope.
Fear will set you free.
You always lose the war with your mind.
Rationality is a delusion.
What you resist persists.
Doubt everything.

Your body never lies.
Love your enemy . . . really.
And to repeat the granddaddy of them all: DON'T FIX
ANYTHING!

Transformational Inquiry translates this paradoxical wisdom into the tools for evolving consciousness developed in this and the following chapters.

DON'T FIX IT!

In the past decade, imaging studies have opened up
the possibility that scientists will soon understand the
mysterious phenomenon [of the placebo effect] and
even harness it in clinical practice—unleashing the
power of, well, nothing.[25]
Erik Vance

The center point around which the tools of Crazy Wisdom nucleate is the paradoxical admonition Don't Fix It! This sounds ludicrous to the Western mind: "What do you mean, don't fix it? Of course we have to fix things; we fix things all the time!" But we can't fix consciousness. The fixing is not ours to do. The Zen teacher, Adyashanti, points to this in the context of enlightenment:

> This inner revolution is the awakening of an intelligence not born of the mind but of an inner silence of mind, which alone has the ability to uproot all of the old structures of one's consciousness. Unless these structures are uprooted, there will be no creative thought, action, or response. Unless there is an inner revolution, nothing new and fresh can flower. Only the old, the repetitious, the conditioned will flower in the absence of this revolution. But our potential lies beyond the known, beyond the structures of the past, beyond anything that humanity has established. Our potential is something that can flower only when we are no longer caught within the influence and limitations of the known. Beyond the realm of the mind, beyond the limitations of humanity's conditioned consciousness, lies that which can be called the sacred. And it is from the sacred that a new

and fluid consciousness is born that wipes away the old and brings to life the flowering of a living and undivided expression of being. Such an expression is neither personal nor impersonal, neither spiritual nor worldly, but rather the flow and flowering of existence beyond all notions of self. [26]

All spiritual traditions point to this inner silence of mind as the access point to deep wisdom. The Eastern traditions emphasize meditation. But we in the West are disinclined to meditation, so think of the adage "Don't Fix It!" as our access point to an inner silence of mind. One pointer toward this understanding comes from the physicist Niels Bohr when he claims that *The opposite of a great truth is not a falsehood, but another great truth.* The point is not to eliminate the opposition, but to stand in the tension (in the inner silence of mind) and allow it to resolve you. This wisdom shows up as the neutralizing third force in Gurdjieff's Law of Three. It is central in the Christian practice of *kenosis*, or self-emptying. *Islam* translates as *surrender* in a similar manner. Buddhism points to *beginner's mind*; Taoism speaks of the *uncarved block*. Socrates claimed, "The only true wisdom is in knowing you know nothing." It is in light of these traditions that "Don't Fix It!" provides the context of the tools presented below.

Even though Immunity to Change is expressed as a practical tool for business, education, and government, it nonetheless enlists this great wisdom. At each step through the four columns, the admonition "Don't Fix It!" guides the way. In the move from a Noble Commitment (Column 1) to the behavior that is thwarting that Commitment (Column 2), "not fixing" is stressed to foster a research orientation. And so it goes throughout the entire process, including tests of the Big Assumptions.

Not fixing is so important for evolving consciousness because it relates to another spiritual truism employed by Transformational Inquiry: *Whatever is brought out of the dark into the light of awareness is transformed.* This is stated beautifully in the Christian tradition: "But everything exposed by the light becomes visible—and everything that is illuminated becomes a light. This is why it is said: 'Wake up, sleeper, rise from the dead, and Christ will shine on you,'"[27] or as some would say, "the Christ will shine within you."

We do not evolve consciousness, consciousness evolves itself. We can participate in this process by attending to what is within, discovering what is blocking the transformative power of consciousness and looking at it. The Crazy Wisdom tools of Transformational Inquiry developed below are all strategies for looking at what blocks the intrinsic intelligence of the universe from flowing through us. Our job is to focus our attention on the invisible impediments of our awakening from one developmental stage to the next and allow the light of awareness to do the heavy lifting. It sounds simple, and it is. It is also one of the most difficult things we will ever engage in because it is anathema to our ego's desire to believe it is separate and independent. I invite you to engage these tools with a spirit of wonder and playfulness. You have nothing to lose but the imaginary prison walls enclosing you.

<hr/>

A Spiritual Frame

Don't Fix It! is another way of practicing mindfulness. It is a core practice of every spiritual tradition. From the perspective of Sofia Perennis, mindfulness opens us to the angel that communicates with our soul and helps our destiny to unfold. In the language of the New Science cosmology, mindfulness engages the silence of discontinuity and permits nonlocal consciousness to do its magic. Finally, using the insights of Jeffrey's Schwartz's work with OCD patients, we begin to rewire our brains as we attach a different sort of value to our complaints.

<hr/>

Tools for Daily Practice

This work is paradoxical: in the following pages I will present a variety of Crazy Wisdom tools from Transformational Inquiry that you can use in your daily life. The thing is, you must not use them to fix anything! As ridiculous as it sounds, these tools will work best if you don't use them to fix things. These tools are all about *not* fixing, because you can't actually fix the things you would like to fix. They are not in your control. However, they can change, and in a direction that will bring you greater freedom, peace and joy. Crazy, huh?

Don't Fix It! is the orientation that energizes all the tools developed in this book. They all derive their power from your willingness to stay in the tension and discomfort of a practice and allow Crazy Wisdom to do its work. So, the first tool to use whenever possible, is to give yourself permission *not* to fix.

This doesn't mean that you shouldn't fix a flat tire on your car, your computer, or leaky faucet. It does mean to *not* fix your spouse, your best friend, the shame you feel for saying something mean, your fear or your rage. Don't Fix It! means to be with the tension of an uncomfortable situation, to not run away from your fear, and to embrace your compulsions. Nifty stuff, huh?

All the tools described below are means for you to *not fix* without being overwhelmed. Each tool brings different insights and addresses different issues. Mix and match them to your heart's content and use the ones that work for you. Turn them into habits then try a few more.

Whining Our Way into Nobility
(Discovering a Noble Commitment)

> "I personally believe we developed language because of
> our deep inner need to complain."
> Jane Wagner

When Kegan and Lahey work in business, government, and educational settings, they invite folks to engage in an important reflection prior to the first meeting. Participants are asked to imagine, or if possible gather, a collection of friends who want the very best for them and ask the following question: "What changes could I make that would make me better at my work, or improve my life in general?" The changes that rank at least a four or five, where five is very important, become the person's Improvement Goals.

Prior to starting a Transformational Inquiry course, I invite folks to engage the same practice. However, at our first in-person meeting, I open with a different kind of conversation. I invite folks to complain. This is a strategy Kegan and Lahey used early in their work but later abandoned because it was tricky to get a good Column 1 Commitment. But it works well in a more exploratory setting, like a small committed group or faith setting. I expand Kegan and Lahey's four-column table to five columns by adding Column 0, Complaints or Frustrations (see Figure 4.1).

COLUMN 0	COLUMN 1	COLUMN 2	COLUMN 3	COLUMN 4
COMPLAINTS OR FRUSTRATIONS	NOBLE COMMITMENT (Improvement Goal)	DOING OR NOT DOING INSTEAD	COMPETING COMMITMENTS	BIG ASSUMPTIONS CORE BELIEFS

Figure 4.1 Adding Complaints or Frustrations to the four-column Immunity to Change matrix

Lightheartedness assists the Inquiry process and creates group cohesion. So, I introduce Column 0 by asking people if they have ever heard of BMW. Some, of course, answer that it means Bavarian Motor Works. "No, no, no," I answer, "you're all wrong! It means Bitch, Moan and Whine! And that's what I'm giving you permission to do, bitch, moan and whine. (How often does that happen?) So pair off and share with one another what really ticks you off, or frustrates you, or if you are more refined you can ask, *What shouldn't be?* Take five minutes to complain then trade partners. Your partner's role is to draw you out and help you complain. Then we share some of our complaints with the larger group."

The key insight of this first step is that we would not complain unless we stood for something. Behind our bitching, moaning and whining is a value system that is typically quite noble. If I complain about something as simple as my roommate not doing the dishes, it may be that the Noble Commitment behind my complaint is grounded in my commitment to being respected or responsible. If I whine about how large corporations dominate our economic and political system, my complaint is likely founded in values of justice, fairness and equal opportunity. As a group, we then translate those values into Noble Commitments or Improvement Goals. My complaint about my roommate not doing the dishes may result in a Noble Commitment to be more respectful to people I disagree with. My dislike of corporate power may result in a Commitment to being more generous with the poor.

It appears that we humans evolved to complain. Our complaint starts with the judgment: "This just shouldn't be!" It can be a complaint about someone we think is doing something they shouldn't. We can bitch about how we feel wronged and poorly served. Or we can simply whine about ourselves, how we are not living up to our expectations. In fact, when the brain is doing the job it evolved to do, it is judging most of the time and complaining a great deal of the time. We think this is bad, but it's entirely normal. But because we judge ourselves as bad when we complain, we diminish ourselves. When we berate ourselves, our self-perception suffers, and we undermine our efficacy by defining ourselves as *whiners*.

As the leader of an Inquiry group, it is important to frame complaints *not* as problems, but as the mind doing *exactly what it is supposed to do!* We are very complex beings. The mind evolved to differentiate, to weigh situations, to notice problems or dangers and consider strategies. The mind judges, it's that simple. We can't stop it, but we can have something to say about how seriously we take the mind's judgments and complaints. It is important to spend some time on this topic. Our culture insists that complaining is bad and that we should not indulge ourselves. As a result we either feel bad for complaining or deny that we are judging. Either strategy effectively removes complaints and judgments from our awareness. When we are not aware of them, they run our lives and we lose access to a valuable lever for change.

Fortunately, simply pointing out the truism that we would not complain unless we stood for something noble can quickly shift our self-perception. In fact, one might argue that without whining and complaining we would never recognize our nobility. A good deal of personal empowerment emerges in this first, simple round of Inquiry. Folks make a subtle, but important, shift from a negative self-image as a complainer and whiner, to someone who stands for something important. This shift serves to embolden folks as we move more deeply into our hidden commitments and Big Assumptions.

⤚⤙

A Spiritual Frame

If our world is made of stories, recognizing the nobility behind our complaints creates a slight, but significant, shift in our personal story. To the degree that I integrate this insight, I begin living into a new story of "me" and create a new world. Within the cosmology of Sofia Perennis, I have encountered a bit of sacred truth that nurtures my awareness. This small insight is a tiny sacred story, precious to God. In the frame of neuroscience, complaints are relabeled as the natural outcome of Noble commitments. Perhaps the brain is being rewired.

⤚⤙

Tools for Daily Practice

When we transition from whiner and complainer to holder of values and Noble Commitments (Column 0 to Column 1) we shift from a victim mindset and a feeling of helplessness to a sense of empowerment. In recognizing that we wouldn't complain unless we stood for something of value, we shift our ideas of ourselves. As a daily practice, when you notice yourself complaining or judging ask yourself, *What value do I hold that leads me to complain?* Then allow yourself to absorb the resulting self-perception.

Damn! Not again!
(Undermining Behaviors)

Behavior is the mirror in which
everyone shows their image.
Johann Wolfgang von Goethe

Having discovered something we would like to change or improve upon (Column 1), it is time to move on to the Column 2 question: "What do I do, or not do, to keep my Noble Commitment from being realized?" That is, what behaviors prevent the realization of my Improvement Goal? Again, this is not about judging ourselves or fixing anything. Quite the opposite! We are on a journey of discovery and this is an essential step along the way. If we get caught up in berating ourselves or trying to change our behaviors, we will miss the deep understanding we are pursuing.

Awareness of what we do *instead* of our Noble Commitments (Column 1 to Column 2) reveals our personal responsibility. The research orientation of Inquiry leads us away from self-recrimination toward curiosity, an essential spiritual practice. Self- recrimination perpetuates the drama of *me*. Curiosity interrupts our preoccupation with ourselves. Instead of berating ourselves for our failures, we ask, *What do my actions reveal about my inner motivations?* Spiritual awakening is furthered whenever that which is subject (has us) becomes an object (what we have), or whenever we are able to bring the light of conscious into the darkness. There are things we would like to do, and goals we would like to achieve. Many of these goals are out of our reach, beyond our control. But often we have some choice, and we make choices that prevent our goals from being realized. The second tool we have is the simple recognition that we may be actively sabotaging the goals we say we want to achieve. Notice that, if you are frustrated about achieving a particular goal or result, you may be part of the problem. If you berate yourself or beat yourself up over your failure, the insight of some personal responsibility will not be a valuable tool for you. If, however, you notice the actions or behaviors that thwart your goal, and *do not judge* those behaviors, you will gain greater understanding and self-acceptance.

Tools for Daily Practice

Your daily practice is to notice any behaviors that impede your goal or Noble Commitment, and simply observe them. Inner commentary may be helpful. When you notice that you have done or said something that thwarts a Noble Commitment simply acknowledge *Ah, I did it again* and move on or forgive yourself as elaborated in the next section.

I REALLY DID MEAN TO HURT YOU
(ACCEPTING JUST THE RIGHT AMOUNT OF RESPONSIBILITY)

If at first you don't succeed, blame your parents.
Marcelene Cox

A vitally important Crazy Wisdom tool emerges in this early stage of Inquiry. It's the idea that *blame is cause for hope*. When I ask folks to identify what they are doing or not doing that keeps their Column 1, Noble Commitment from being realized, I am asking them to take personal responsibility for their behavior. Our culture teaches us to either take *full* responsibility for our behaviors or find enough excuses to totally justify them, but neither extreme is realistic or useful. On the one hand, we are never fully responsible. We are constrained and shaped by any number of factors beyond our control: our genetic inheritance, our gender, our social institutions, our culture, and our income, to name just a few. At the same time, we are never completely without choice.

The tool that emerges here is not part of the Immunity to Change process but comes from my experience in a transformational group more than four decades ago run by Wallace and Edna McAfee. The essential insight is that, no matter how little or much free will we truly have, any free choice is a reason for hope and a powerful tool for evolving consciousness. But we must work with it carefully. For free will not only implies choice, it infers blame. If we choose poorly with whatever amount of free will we might have, we are responsible for the outcomes of that choice, and we are to blame if it comes out badly. When I accept blame, and the shame that accompanies it, my self-protective mechanisms come into play. Blame and shame can readily shut me down and keep me from exploring any further. Self-discovery and personal evolution cease.

The remedy is to follow a vitally important axiom: *claim no more blame then you can accept forgiveness for*. If you believe you have abundant free will yet still make poor, cruel, or vindictive choices, the remorse and blame you feel can overwhelm you and trigger retreat. I encourage individuals to give themselves lots of excuses for their actions, to actively blame their actions on all kinds of external forces, but always find some free choice. I then insist that they accept forgiveness for their freely chosen behaviors. Whether they envision forgiveness coming from God, the universe, their parents, their friends, or themselves, I insist that they accept forgiveness for their free choice *before moving ahead*. If they cannot fully accept forgiveness for their choice, then they need to take on less free will.

The power, and the danger, of this wisdom are implied in the title of this section: *I Really Did Mean to Hurt You*. Most of us don't want to admit that we freely choose to hurt another individual. Everything in our culture says this is wrong. But when we look within, we often discover that, yes, we did really want to hurt that person. Now, I may not have had much choice in causing that harm. I might be in a job that requires me to take hurtful actions, like firing people. I may have been raised in an abusive family and confused love and abuse at an early age. I may be short-tempered because I'm in chronic pain. All of these are real and valid excuses for why I might hurt you. In fact these, and other largely uncontrollable factors, might account for 99 percent of my hurtful actions leaving me to claim only 1 percent free will. But even 1 percent is reason for hope. But first I must recognize, and accept, that I freely chose to hurt you. Generally we don't want to accept even this amount of responsibility. However, it is essential we claim the blame, and the shame, associated with our choice without wallowing in it. We do this by accepting forgiveness (from whatever source) for our freely chosen actions.

Accepting blame is straight forward. It's as easy as acknowledging to yourself (or others) that, yes, I meant to cause harm or hurt in this realm where I had choice. But from what we accept forgiveness depends upon our understanding of life, our cosmology. If you believe there is only one God, we can ask forgiveness from him or her. If you come from a non-dual faith you can tap into the forgiveness intrinsic to being. If you are more secular in your orientation, you may ask forgiveness from a friend, or imagine someone forgiving you. The challenge is in receiving that forgiveness. Receiving requires a kind of surrender, a letting down of barriers, an openness. It is an act of vulnerability that is difficult for the ego to endure.

You have perhaps heard the adage "What you resist, persists." As long as we resist acknowledging a mistake or a harmful act, it remains lodged in our awareness. It becomes a hurdle that blocks our progress because we avoid going down certain paths of thought and feeling that will bring us in touch with the part of ourselves we are seeking to deny. The act of accepting forgiveness (from whatever source) effectively eliminates the hurdle and simultaneously expands our arena of choice. By becoming aware of that which we have so energetically denied, we turn it from *subject* to *object*, precisely the action which defines evolving consciousness.

A Spiritual Frame

Forgiveness is central to the Christian cosmology. Even though we have not focused on it in our different cosmologies, it is a central tenet of Christianity as well as the world's other faith traditions. ("Do unto others as you would have them do unto you," and all its variations exist across traditions).

From the neuropsychological point of view, we reduce the free will we must accept when we relabel many of our actions as compulsive behaviors of the mind, re-attribute our actions to an addictive brain, and give ourselves great excuses for our behavior. All of these actions help us reduce our free will to something we can accept forgiveness for.

Tools for Daily Practice

Here is the essence of this tool: first, give yourself plenty of excuses for the behavior that thwarted your Noble Commitment, but always find a realm of free choice, no matter how small. Second, claim just the amount of blame commensurate with your immediate willingness to accept forgiveness.

Most of us have ample opportunity to practice this throughout the day. There are always things we would have preferred to do differently. It might be making a nasty comment, cutting someone off in traffic, or simply judging someone based on their looks. Allow yourself plenty of excuses, but find a realm of choice and immediately accept forgiveness.

As a daily practice, simply notice when you screw up. If you're like me, you fall short of your best self many times each day. Every falling short is a little opportunity to evolve your consciousness. First, acknowledge that you fell short of your expectations. Then consider to what degree you're falling short was excusable. There might have been lots of external circumstances that caused you to screw up. But be sure to find some area in which you could have chosen differently and you didn't. Then open yourself and accept forgiveness for your bad choice. Then move on.

Say, for example, you made a cruel remark to a fellow worker. Your first impulse is to push the act out of awareness, which is just the brain doing its job. Feel free to give yourself lots of excuses for being mean: you didn't sleep well last night, you drank too much coffee, your partner was angry at you this morning, etc. But don't excuse it all the way! Take some blame for being an ass. Once you've accepted some blame and responsibility, avoid fixing it. Don't waste your time resolving not to be snotty again. It won't work! Instead, seek forgiveness from God, the universe, yourself, an imaginary friend, or maybe even the person you insulted. *Then allow it in!* If your internal dialogue goes something like, *Okay, I was an ass. I could've done it differently, but I didn't. I am ashamed and sorry. Please forgive me.* Then you are on the right track. Now accept forgiveness. Over time you will notice this practice becoming easier and easier. You will notice that you screw up, acknowledge it, accept forgiveness, and move on.

If you hold regrets, if some scenes keep replaying in your mind, you have probably avoided your share of responsibility and the healing that comes with forgiveness. You can bring this dynamic of blame and forgiveness to that regret. Simply recall the incident that brings you anguish, compile your excuses, find your area of personal responsibility, ask forgiveness, and open yourself to receiving it. Period.

Here's a more subtle example: let's say you are white, and you just noticed that you mentally judged a black man walking into the room (good job catching the thought!). Assume that you have myriad great excuses: you live in a racist society, your parents were not very accepting of blacks, your culture portrays black men as dangerous, and you once had a scary encounter with a black man. Yet you also notice that you could have reacted differently: you could have stopped the bigoted story running in your head, but instead you indulged. Accept blame and responsibility for not stopping your prejudicial story and immediately accept forgiveness from whatever source works for you. Notice that when you look at your blame it always feels like 100%, but it's not. It is really very small. But no matter how small, it is still cause for hope. Accepting both blame and forgiveness may sound something like this: *Oh look, I did it again, I let my prejudice run loose and when I could have tried to cut it off. Ouch!* Then open yourself to receive forgiveness.

That's the ideal. As you practice over time it will become easier and easier. Other times, your mind will latch on to your blame and dwell on it. You will want to run away, we all do. But stay with it. First, give yourself more excuse, reduce the amount of blame you are trying to take on. Our minds are so deeply conditioned, nearly any excuse you come up with will be based in truth. Be generous with yourself! Once you have gotten your blame to a manageable level (but not zero), envision being forgiven. Feel yourself being loved and accepted unconditionally; cherished, even when you willfully did harm. Find a source for this unconditional love, be it a parent, God, the universe, your higher self, or just a felt sense. Let this forgiveness sustain you until your blame and shame pass, which it will if you do not feed it with guilt.

chapter 5

hidden motivations

The next two tools, *What, Me Worry?* and *Where Did You Come From?*, work together to uncover motivations hidden from our conscious awareness. I have paired them because together they illuminate our Competing Commitments (Column 3) and reveal our dynamic Immunity to Change. They both offer different practices you can use on a daily basis to remove blockages to the radiant awareness that wants to blossom in you.

WHAT, ME WORRY?
(LIBERATING ANXIETIES)

The real voyage of discovery consists in not seeking new landscapes, but in having new eyes.
Marcel Proust

Anxiety is the hand maiden of creativity.
T. S. Eliot

As we take the next step in the Immunity to Change process, moving from Column 2 to Column 3, I ask participants to take a deep breath, close their eyes, and remember one time during the week when they did something, or avoided doing something, that prevented their Noble Commitments from being realized. Once they have a clear picture of these behaviors, they are invited to imagine doing the opposite and notice what anxieties arise. *What are your anxieties? Where are they felt in the body? Is there an image or scene associated with each anxiety? What do you envision happening if you do the opposite of their Column 2 behavior?* After opening their eyes, folks are invited to take a minute and silently record their images or sensations in the Worry Box at the top of Column 3. I encourage everyone to express their anxieties in the most raw and primitive form they can muster. After a few minutes of personal reflection, everyone shares with their partners.

This step can be tricky, so let me share a personal experience. I have used Inquiry very effectively to lose weight and keep it off. As you might imagine, my Noble Commitment was to lose X number of pounds. The behavior that thwarted this commitment was my craving for sugar. I love sugary pastries of any kind; add butter and it's pure heaven. I found it extremely difficult to pass up anything sugar-coated or infused with sugar. When I imagined doing the opposite, that is, not eating a sugary treat, I would go into a near panic. This is partly a physiological response to sugar addiction. But the physical craving for sugar diminishes rapidly over a few days of abstinence and this I could achieve by will power. The psychological dimension was much harder to handle. When I imagined not eating a pastry, I got anxious. This was the material for my Worry Box. So, when I considered doing the opposite of my Column 2 behaviors, not having sugary treats, my anxiety was that I would feel deeply deprived and that my cravings would overwhelm me, and even that my brain would go into low gear and I wouldn't be able to think clearly. (See Figure 5.1)

WHERE DID YOU COME FROM?
(UNCOVERING OUR COMPETING COMMITMENTS)

Our next step is to translate worries and anxieties from our Worry Box into Competing Commitments. Competing Commitments flow directly from the anxieties recorded in the Worry Box. Often, the words used in the Worry Box will translate into good Competing Commitments. Based on my anxiety about feeling deprived if I didn't have sugary snacks, my Competing Commitment was *I may also be committed to never feeling deprived.* Another useful way to say this is *I may also be committed to always having things my way!* Also, I may also be committed to. . . *Not being overwhelmed.* Or, in different language, *being in control.* The sign of a good Competing Commitment is that it is self-serving and not something you'd likely share with the world. Being committed to never being deprived, always having your own way, or being in control all qualify as self-serving.

At this point, our personal Immunity to Change reveals itself. Even though we genuinely hold a Noble Commitment, or improvement goal, we are thwarted in the realization of that goal by a hidden, self-serving Competing Commitment. Given our Column 3 Competing Commitment, our Column 2 behavior makes perfect sense. In fact, it is a brilliant response to this hidden commitment. (See Figure 5.1)

COLUMN 1	COLUMN 2	COLUMN 3	COLUMN 4
NOBLE COMMITMENT (Improvement Goal)	DOING OR NOT DOING INSTEAD	COMPETING COMMITMENTS	BIG ASSUMPTIONS CORE BELIEFS
Lose X pounds	•I eat sugary treats **Dynamic Immunity to Change**	***Worry Box*** •I'll feel deprived •My cravings will overwhelm me •I won't be able to think __Competing Commitments__ I may also be committed to... ...not feeling deprived ...having things my way, NOW! ...not being overwhelmed ...being in control	

Figure 5.1. Our Dynamic Immunity to Change

Not only do we prevent ourselves from making the change we say we want to make, our Immunity to Change is dynamic. If we move toward our improvement goals, our anxieties (in the Worry Box) increase and draw us into our hidden self-serving Competing Commitments. On the other hand, when we indulge our invisible Competing Commitments, we eventually grow frustrated with ourselves and pledge anew to our Noble Commitment. We wobble back and forth between our invisible Competing Commitments and our Noble Commitments, never strayed far from our Column 2 behaviors.

In my example, my desire to lose weight is counter-balanced by my commitment to consume sugary snacks and to not feeling deprived. Using will power, I was able to stay away from sugary snacks for a while. But the longer I stayed away, the more my anxiety increased, until finally, my resolve was nibbled away and I gave in. This set off a period of indulgence that eventually caused enough guilt and discomfort to resurrect my Noble Commitment and my resolve to *change it this time!* All the while, my Column 2 behaviors wobbled around the same general dynamic which kept my weight about the same.

☙ ❧

A Spiritual Frame

"What, Me Worry?" is another one of those Crazy Wisdom insights. By considering doing the opposite of the behaviors that thwart my Noble Commitment, I enlist the wisdom of my body and start the dive into a hidden realm that has more power over me than I would like to acknowledge. By moving in the direction of my fears and anxieties, I engage the ancient wisdom that my fears are the door to my freedom. From the Christian liturgical year, I am engaging Lent; the shadow side of myself that I would prefer to avoid. According to the Gospel of Thomas, I am entering "trouble" with my eyes wide open. From the cosmology of Sofia Perennis, by engaging my fears and anxieties, I open to the soul deepening stories inspired by the divine to help create order out of chaos.

"Where Did You Come From?" reveals our dynamic of our Immunity to Change. This is expressed classically in the Christian tradition by St. Paul: "I do not understand what I do. For what I want to do I do not do, but what I hate I do. . . . As it is, it is no longer I myself who do it, but it is sin living in me. For I know that good itself does not dwell in me, that is, in my sinful nature. For I have the desire to do what is good, but I cannot carry it out." (Romans 7:15–18). "Sin" points directly to the complex interactions of our Noble and Competing Commitments that keep our immunities to change below our awareness.

Drawing on the insights of neuropsychologist Jeffrey Schwartz, by relabeling our anxieties as self-protective Competing Commitments essential to our self-preservation, we gain distance from them, and potentially a new relationship to them.

The Law of Three highlights, as a universal law of evolution, how we can get stuck in the polarity of "affirming" and "denying" a polarity that is only resolved by a third, "neutralizing," force.

☙ ❧

Tools for Daily Practice

"What, Me Worry?" takes us into territory we prefer to avoid. When we move from Column 2 to Column 3 in the Immunity to Change process we ask, "If I imagine doing the opposite of my Column 2 behavior, what anxiety arises?" We use this question as a tool for deeper exploration, but it has great value in its own right. We typically don't want to acknowledge the fear, anxieties or discomforts that arise if we imagine trying something different. We push it back from our awareness where we can't see it or question into it, so it runs us. Thus, our next tool for daily use is simply this: when you notice an activity that stymies your stated goal or Noble Commitment, imagine doing the opposite and simply notice what anxieties arise for you. Do not criticize or berate yourself, rather allow yourself to sit in the anxiety, to feel it, and to observe how it arises and then falls away.

Where Did You Come From? invites you to probe deeper. Ask yourself, *What else might I also be committed to?* Again, sit with whatever arises within you. Finally see if you can watch the dynamic push and pull of your immunity to change system as it unfolds throughout the day. Watch its patterns and power; see how it keeps you stuck in particular habits. As always, try not to judge, stop, or fix this dynamic. Smile at what you see, embrace it, love it if you can.

GETTING TO KNOW YOU
(INTERVIEWING OUR COMPETING COMMITMENTS)

Until you make the unconscious conscious, it will direct
your life and you will call it fate.
C.G. Jung

Man is not what he thinks he is, he is what he hides.
André Malraux

Having uncovered the self-protective Competing Commitments that run our lives below our conscious awareness (in the dynamic immunity to change that keeps us stuck), we can now take steps to loosen their grip by getting to know them. In the following two sections I lay out a variety of tools you can use to befriend your Competing Commitments and inspired fundamental changes in your life.

We begin simply by interviewing our Competing Commitments. We break into pairs and interview one another as we inhabit the very different selves within us.

Instructions

Pair off with a partner. You will take turns interviewing one another and playing the role of the Noble Commitment. (Interview questions are listed below.) The partner playing the Noble Commitment is questioned by their partner. When you are being interviewed as the Noble Commitment, shift your posture to reflect the feeling of your Noble Commitment. When you are the interviewer, ask the following questions, then listen carefully without comments or opinions. Do not give advice or try to fix anything.

Taking the Role of the Noble Commitment

The *interviewer* asks the following questions of the Noble Commitment:
Please tell me your name.
(Response: This can be as simple as, *I am the Noble Commitment*, or the interviewee can give his or her Noble Commitment a name).
What do you stand for? Please elaborate.
Why is this important to you?
If you lived more fully into this Noble Commitment, how would you act in the world?
What are the values behind this Noble Commitment?
Tell me why these are important to you.
Is there anything else you would like to tell me?
(You may ask additional questions as long as they are open-ended.)

Now switch roles and repeat the questions. Once both partners have interviewed each other in the role of the Noble Commitment, come back and share with the larger group. We often ask the interviewer to tell about their partner in the role of the Noble Commitment. We then ask the interviewee how it felt to be in that role and to be interviewed.

We now move on to interview the Competing Commitments (Column 3). We return to our previous partners. Again the interviewee, the one playing the role of the self-protective Competing Commitment, is asked to change their posture to represent this Commitment. The interviewer continues to ask open-ended, exploratory questions without leading the interviewee. We return to similar interview questions.

TAKING THE ROLE OF THE COMPETING COMMITMENT

The *interviewer* asks the following question of the Competing Commitment:

Please tell me your name.

(Response: This can be as simple as, *I am a Competing Commitment*, or the interviewee can give his or her Competing Commitment a name).

What is your role in [person's name] life? Please elaborate.

Why is it important that you do this job?

If you didn't do this job, what might happen? Please elaborate

And if that happened, what might happen next? . . . And next? . . . Next?

(These questions invite the interviewee to tell the story of his or her Big Assumptions behind their self-protective commitments).

Why does this matter to you?

Is there anything else you would like to tell me?

(You may ask additional questions as long as they are open-ended.)

This interview has a very different tenor than the first. Expect it to take longer than the previous one. When both partners have interviewed one another, return to the larger circle and report as before.

It is important for the facilitator to prevent the conversation from deteriorating into strategies to fix things. We are not in the business of fixing anything! In fact, our motivation is to do precisely the opposite; allow individuals to experience these different aspects of themselves in a safe, loving environment. The most natural thing in the world for us to do is to help one another get out of our distress. But this does not serve us. To restate a fundamental premise of this work: our Competing Commitments and Big Assumptions cause problems for us because we never look at them long enough to allow them to change. Fixing is functionally a way to re-bury our distressing Competing Commitments. Small groups give participants time and support to look at the thoughts and feelings that bring discomfort. In this looking, the distressing emotions associated with our Competing Commitments are allowed to run their lifecycle, to be felt, and to dissipate. It is important for individuals to experience this routinely through the process of Transformational Inquiry.

A Spiritual Frame

In the Christian frame of the liturgical year, we are again engaging the season of Lent as we dive into the shadows of our "sin" (heart dynamic immunity

to change). From the orientation of the Gospel of Thomas, we are working on the transition from trouble to that of wonder. As we investigate those parts of ourselves we have denied but have discovered in our process of seeking, we can only wonder at their power and come to reign over them in the openhearted act of self-emptying (kenosis).

And again we encounter forgiveness. Without judging, but only inquiring, we embrace our profound complexity.

<hr/>

Tools for Daily Practice

When we redefine the fears and anxieties listed in the Worry Box as self-protective Competing Commitments we begin to recast them as allies, allies helping us to avoid a hell we believe could destroy us. We are no longer at war with our fears but begin to recognize them as responses arising from a part of us seeking to protect us from dire consequences.

As a regular practice, whenever you can notice a Competing Commitment in action, briefly interview it. Ask what it is protecting you from and why it is important. Do not judge or argue with the answer you receive. Simply thank your self-protective Competing Commitment and move on. This whole process will require only a minute or so of your time.

FALLING IN LOVE AGAIN
(THE PRACTICE OF PSYCHODRAMA)

We can never obtain peace in the outer world until we make peace with ourselves.
Dalai Lama XIV

The essence of psychodrama is role-playing, quite simply taking the role of another. In Transformational Inquiry, we use psychodrama in a very simple form. We place a card table in the middle of the room with a chair on either side. The individual (Participant) who wants to work on an issue sits on one side, and their Support Person sits on the other. As indicated in the drawing, the person role-playing the Noble Commitment (NC) always sits in one chair, and the individual taking the role of the self-protective Competing Commitment (CC) takes the opposite chair. The table serves the ritualistic function of informing everyone that a psychodrama is in

Graphic 5.1: Setting Up Psychodrama

process. The alter egos are there to support and encourage both individuals in their different roles. Psychodrama for Transformational Inquiry uses three rounds.

ROUND 1: RELEASE

Round 1 is about experiencing and releasing emotions. Our Participant sits in the chair of their Column 1 Noble Commitment (NC). In this first round they are encouraged to express their frustration and anger at the Column 3, self-protective Competing Commitment (CC) that is stifling their efforts to achieve their goals. The alter-egos are played by individuals from the surrounding group who support the Participant's efforts to express their anger and frustration. Participants sitting in the role of Noble Commitment are often hesitant to express their frustration and anger. Since folks in the alter ego roles are slightly detached, they can often express feelings the Participants would not be comfortable sharing. Below is a very short sample dialogue. (A full transcript of an individual psychodrama, without the group, is presented in appendix C). As you will see, a typical round 1 psychodrama would typically go longer and get more heated:

Participant (in the role of the Column 1 Noble Commitment): "I'm tired of trying to please everyone! I want to stop, but you keep getting in my way!"

Support (Column 3 Competing Commitment): "But you can't stop! We have to keep people happy. That's our job!"

Graphic 5.2: Set Up for Round 1

Participant: "No it's not! I don't want to please everyone! I just want to please myself."

Support: "Oh, you don't understand. Really (pleading), you don't understand! If you don't please everyone, it will be just awful! What if you didn't keep mom happy? You'd just die!"

Alter-ego 1 (supporting the Participant): "Bullshit! All you ever do is make me feel guilty. You get in my way, then get in my way again, and then you get in my way again! Get the hell out of my life!"

Participant (with considerable feeling): "Yeah! Get the hell out of my way!" Slapping the table: "I want you out of my life!"

This is a good result. Any release on the part of our Participant opens the door to greater willingness to listen to the Competing Commitment.

ROUND 2: JUSTIFYING OUR COMPETING COMMITMENTS

For Round 2, our actors change chairs. Our Support Person has moved into the role of the Noble Commitment (NC), and our Participant is in the role of the Competing Commitment (CC).

Changing chairs is important, not only for tracking the different roles, but to help the actors shift their perspectives. The opportunity in Round 2 is for our Participant to take the role of the self-protective Competing

Graphic 5.3: Set Up for Round 2

Commitment (CC) and begin to understand its perspective. Until now, the dominant lens of the Participant has been the Noble Commitment (NC). The Competing Commitment (CC) has typically been seen as the enemy or hindrance. In this round, our Participant inhabits the role of the Competing Commitment to explain its point of view. I often ask the Participant to overplay the role to help them begin to identify with it. Here is another short dialogue:

Support *(in the role of the Noble Commitment):* "You again! Okay, let's see what you have to say for yourself."

Participant *(in the role of the Competing Commitment):* "Please hear me. You've got to listen to me! I am trying to protect you from a horrible catastrophe! I'm not trying to keep you from your wonderful, noble goals; I'm trying to protect you from the greatest disaster of your life. We really have to pay attention to keeping the people around us, the people that are significant in our lives—everyone—happy. If we don't, we'll end up completely alone! If our friends and family aren't happy, they'll leave us. We'll be on our own, with no one to rely on, with no one to love us. Why don't you understand!?"

Support *(as NC):* "You're a basket case! Okay, I'm listening. Tell me why we have to make everyone happy?"

Participant *(as CC):* "Don't you remember when mom left? She used to take care of us; she was there to hold us when we were hurt or upset. It probably would've been easier if she had died, but she didn't, she just left!

Dad tried, I know, but it wasn't the same. He had to work. He didn't know how to be a mom. God, it hurt so much! Maybe if mom had been happier she wouldn't have left. We can't take that chance again! I wouldn't survive.

Support *(as NC)*: "I see" (big sigh). "You're really scared, aren't you?"

Participant *(as CC)*: "Yes, yes! You finally heard me!"

It's not unusual for this to be a profoundly emotional time for our Participant. This may be the first time they have glimpsed their own hidden, self-protective Competing Commitment. Even in this abbreviated encounter, you can the sense its power. Not only are painful memories likely to come up but it may be the first time the self-protective Competing Commitment has been acknowledged. This initiates a significant opening for Round 3.

ROUND 3: FORGIVENESS

The focus of Round 3 is empathy and forgiveness. Our Participant now moves back into the seat of the Noble Commitment (NC). In this round, the Participant's task is to reach out to his or her self-protective Competing Commitment (CC) with care and understanding. It helps to invite the Participant to see the Competing Commitment as a frightened young child. I ask our Participant to reach out and touch the hand of the Support person in the role of the Competing Commitment. The job of the Participant in the role of the Noble commitment is to both understand the perspective of the

Graphic 5.4: Set Up for Round 3

Competing Commitment (CC) and to forgive him- or herself as necessary. The Support Person in the role of self-protective Competing Commitment more or less repeats what our Participant had articulated in the previous round. You might imagine that our Participant, just having played the role of the self-protective Competing Commitment, would be unfazed by hearing what they themselves had just articulated. In my experience, this has never been the case. It's almost like our Participant is hearing his or her self-protective Competing Commitment for the first time. The insights can be profound. Here is another short dialogue:

Support (*in the role of the Competing Commitment*): "You've gotta hear me! If we don't keep the people around us happy, we're in horrible danger! I'm terrified we'll end up alone and miserable if we don't keep these folks happy."

Participant (*as the Noble Commitment*): "You're terrified aren't you? You really believe if we offend someone, or don't do what they ask, that they'll leave us."

Support (*as CC*): "Yes! Yes! That's exactly it! I'm so scared. I do everything I can to protect us but you couldn't care less!"

Participant (*as NC*): "I'm so sorry, I had no idea! I thought you were just being a pain in the butt, but you're really trying to protect me, aren't you?"

Support (*as CC*): "Of course! How could you think anything else? I'm so afraid for us. Just imagine if Susie or Bob stopped liking us. If they turned away from us, it would just be the beginning. Before you knew it, all of our friends, everyone we care about, would be gone. Oh! We'd be so lonely and miserable. I'd die!"

Participant (*as NC*): "Oh sweetheart, you're really on my side aren't you? You're trying to protect us in every way you can, and I'm fighting you every inch of the way. I think I'm beginning to understand. I'm sorry."

As you can imagine, it is profoundly touching to watch from the support role as realization dawns on the Participant's face.

In psychodrama we not only bring our Competing Commitments and Big Assumptions out of the shadows, we dance with them. We engage them in a way that allows them to change. Forgive the personification, but when the inspiring Noble Commitment finally greets the self-protective Competing Commitment with caring and empathy, fear evaporates, at least temporarily. In a new atmosphere of safety, the internal persona of the Competing Commitment can loosen its grip on the Big Assumptions that have guided it. The new insights of the Noble Commitment allow it to lessen its hostile stance toward the Competing Commitment. And the dynamic Immunity to Change between the Column 1 (Noble Commitment) and the Column 3 (Competing Commitment) loosens its grip. It may not fall away completely, but the loosening permits a deeper investigation of the

Big Assumptions behind the self-protective Competing Commitment. In this new, safer environment, the persona of the self-protective Competing Commitment can listen more openly to challenges of the Big Assumption that come from Safe Tests and other techniques.

❧

A Spiritual Frame

Not only does psychodrama draw on the ancient spiritual admonition to forgive, it also highlights the technique that neuropsychologist Jeffrey Schwartz uses to get his OCD patients to relabel their compulsions. In the process of psychodrama we relabel our self-protective Commitment as a friend. We develop a different relationship to it. Through the lens of the Law of Three, the Noble Commitment represents the "first" force, active or affirming; our Competing Commitment represents the "second," force, denying. Forgiveness is the neutralizing, "third" force that engenders a new, emergent resolution. Of course, the three rounds of psychodrama used here are also consistent with the Buddhist understanding that the world, our world, is made of stories. As we change the story of our relationship with our Competing Commitments, we change our world.

❧

Tools for Daily Practice

Even though psychodrama is practiced in pairs, no one is left out. Observers will often report meaningful, and powerful, insights emerging while merely watching a psychodrama. These folks are generally as engaged in the process as the Participants. But the transformative power of psychodrama goes well beyond the event. Below are some very practical tools for daily use.

Release. Round 1 is about release. The idea is to get really mad at the hidden self-protective Competing Commitment (Column 3) that is frustrating your efforts to achieve your goal (Column 1). On your own, you are invited to feel your frustration and express your anger. As a regular practice, allow yourself to vocalize your frustration (Not in public! The car is a great place!). Yell at your Competing Commitment; tell it why you are so frustrated. Yelling helps clarify both your Noble Commitment (Column1) and the Competing Commitment (Column 3). And it feels really good!

Justifying your actions. In Round 2 you take the role of the Competing Commitment (Column 3) and justify your actions. When you feel stressed or anxious, your task is to explain to the Noble Commitment (Column 1) what you are protecting it from. Express as clearly and simply as possible the danger that looms ahead if the Column 1 goal is pursued.

Write it down, or say it aloud! The point is to enter the mindset of the Competing Commitment as deeply as possible. After all, the self-protective Competing Commitment is you. It genuinely, and innocently, seeks the best for your life.

Empathy and forgiveness. Round 3 focuses on empathy and forgiveness. Returning to the role of the Noble Commitment, your task is to reach out to your Competing Commitment (Column 3) with caring and understanding. As a practice, see your Competing Commitment as a frightened young child (you) that you want to comfort. Hear what the child is saying to you. Acknowledge his or her fear and the genuine desire to protect you. See yourself embracing that child. Hold him or her in your arms and assure them they are safe. Do not argue with the way they see the world or in any way suggest that their fear is misplaced. Only hold them and let them know that they are loved and accepted just as they are. Treat this internal child just as you would any frightened child, hold them and comfort them so they can feel the safety of your love. Invite the child to speak their fears as clearly as possible and simply receive those fears with a welcome embrace and unconditional love. You will be delighted to discover how this innocent child responds. Somewhat differently, try seeing this young child as a good friend who is trying to protect you. Invite him or her to tell you about the danger and listen without judgment.

chapter 6
into the depths

Truth is a jealous, vicious mistress that
never, ever sleeps.
Tahereh Mafi

Having become better acquainted with our self-protective Competing Commitments, it is time to dive into the source of those Commitments, our Big Assumptions. These are the Core Beliefs that *have us*. Our objective in the following practices is to gently question the truth of those Core Beliefs without scaring ourselves. This sounds a bit odd, but most of us have spent decades nurturing our ignorance about the Big Assumptions that run our lives. Nurturing our ignorance is both a passive and active process that has been incredibly successful. On the passive side, our Big Assumptions create filters that prevent us from seeing the Big Assumptions that created the filters in the first place. More actively, we avoid questioning into our Core Beliefs because our identity is founded upon them. Our brain perceives inquiry as a threat and leads us away. So the following tools are intended to keep our Big Assumptions right at the edge of our awareness. We don't want them staring us in the face where they can overwhelm us, nor do we want to bury them where they become invisible again. Our first step is to dive in to our invisible Big Assumptions from the platform of our Competing Commitments.

In the 4-column Immunity to Change sequence I ask people to state their Competing Commitments in the rawest language possible. In my personal example from an earlier chapter, when I envisioned forgoing a yummy sweet, I would feel my anxiety rise and watch as my mind made up all kinds of justifications for having a snack. The rawest statement of my Competing Commitment was *I want it now!* This was accompanied by a vision of myself as a two-year-old throwing a tantrum on the floor crying, "I want it now! I want it now!" That ends up being a pretty good statement of my Competing Commitment; when it comes to a sugary snack, I am committed to having it NOW! This is a good platform for diving into Big Assumptions.

DIVING IN!
(UNCOVERING BIG ASSUMPTIONS)

As it is, the lover of inquiry must follow his beloved
wherever it may lead him.
Plato

There are two effective pathways into our hidden Big Assumptions. First, we can ask *What assumptions must I be holding to have this Competing Commitment?* and then list these in Column 4. Another avenue is to consider doing the inverse of the Competing Commitment and complete the statement, *I assume that if I did the opposite of my self-protective Competing Commitment, then* . . . and complete the sentence. Folks are asked to take some time alone to make the transition from their Column 3 Competing Commitments to their Big Assumptions and then to follow their Big Assumptions as far as they can by continuing to ask, *and then?* . . . *and then?*. . . The next step is to share with a partner. We return to the larger group with volunteers sharing their insights.

In my example: I assumed that if I didn't get my snack NOW that my craving would increase dramatically; I'd go into a sugar crash; my craving would overwhelm me; and I would be miserable for the rest of my life. So I might as well die now! This is a typical, good Big Assumption: it is dire and somewhat absurd. The rational mind looks at this and says it's ridiculous, yet it has profound emotional impact. Notice that the Column 3 Competing Commitment is a *necessary* response to this Big Assumption; if I unconsciously assume that these dire things will happen if I don't get my snack then, *of course*, I'll have a deep commitment to getting my snack NOW! My behavior of eating sugary snacks flies in direct opposition to my Noble Commitment of losing weight. (See Figure 6.1.)

COLUMN 1	COLUMN 2	COLUMN 3	COLUMN 4
NOBLE COMMITMENT (Improvement Goal)	DOING OR NOT DOING INSTEAD	COMPETING COMMITMENTS	BIG ASSUMPTIONS CORE BELIEFS
Lose X pounds	• I eat sugary treats	***Worry Box*** • I'll feel deprived • My cravings will overwhelm me • I won't be able to think **Competing Commitments** I may also be committed to... ...not feeling deprived ...having things my way, NOW! ...not being overwhelmed ...being in control	• I assumed that if I didn't get my snack NOW... • my craving will increase dramatically. • I'll to go into a sugar crash; and my craving will overwhelm me. • I will be miserable for the rest of my life. • I might as well die now!

Figure 6.1: Adding Big Assumptions to the food example.

A Spiritual Frame

When we say that the world is made of stories, we are exploring our Big Assumptions. The complex of Big Assumptions operating beneath our conscious awareness constitutes the fundamental stories that create our lives. Our hidden Core Beliefs create the structure of our world; they create the filters through which knowledge enters and exclude that which does not conform to our story of self.

In the language of the Gospel of Thomas, once we find we will be troubled. We will be troubled to find that so much of our life is directed by a matrix of beliefs often formed during early childhood and not questioned since. In the Christian liturgical year, this continues the season of Lent, diving into our deepest shadows as an essential step in our awakening.

Tools for Daily Practice

When we dive into our Big Assumptions (Column 3 to Column 4), we begin to uncover a hidden universe of unexamined Core Beliefs. This transition opens the door to profound self-examination that works by slowly uncovering a vast matrix of assumptions and beliefs that have likely run our lives for decades. To begin accessing our hidden Big Assumptions we consider doing the opposite of our Competing Commitments and explore *I assume that if I did the opposite, then . . .* and follow the Big Assumption Story as deeply as possible.

A simplified version of this process is to ask, when I notice I am avoiding a particular action, "what must I be assuming about the consequences of this action?" In the following sections I will offer more elaborate tools for inquiring into Big Assumptions, but this simple question can be surprisingly effective to maintain moment-by-moment awareness.

THE ELEPHANT'S IN CHARGE
(OUR BIG ASSUMPTIONS IN ACTION)

Elephants rule, although they are sometimes open to persuasion by riders.
Jonathan Haidt

The title for this section comes from a marvelous book by Jonathan Haidt entitled *The Righteous Mind: Why Good People Are Divided by Politics and Religion.*[28] His description of how "*intuitions come first, strategic reasoning second*" aptly describes our relationship with our Big Assumptions. Haidt begins with a confession: "On February 3, 2007, shortly before lunch, I discovered that I was a chronic liar." His wife had just asked him not to leave dirty dishes on the counter in a tone he interpreted as: "as I have asked you 100 times before." His full description bears repeating:

> . . . So there I was at my desk, writing about how people automatically fabricate justifications of their gut feelings, when suddenly I realized that I had just done the same thing with my wife. I disliked being criticized, and I had felt a flash of negativity by the time Jayne had gotten to her third word ("*Can you not. . .*"). Even before I knew why she was criticizing me, I knew I disagreed with her (because intuitions come first). The instant I knew the content of the

criticism *(". . . leave dirty dishes on the. . .")*, my inner lawyer went to work searching for an excuse (strategic reasoning second). It's true that I had eaten breakfast, given Max his first bottle, and let Andy out for his first walk, but these events had all happened at separate times. Only when my wife criticized me did I merge them into a composite image of a harried father with too few hands, and I created this fabrication by the time she had completed her one sentence criticism *(". . . counter where I make baby food?")*. I then lied so quickly and convincingly that my wife and I both believed me.[29]

Our Big Assumption Story is often, though not always, the source of our intuitions, our gut feelings. Our Big Assumption Story *is* the elephant in the room. Our Big Assumptions are not just thoughts, they comprise an entire mental-emotional complex shaping our reality moment by moment. Our intellect, the rider on the elephant, is usually the last to know what's going on and, as Haidt explains, mostly relegated to making excuses for the elephant's actions. Transforming consciousness requires that we begin observing the shenanigans of our Big Assumption elephant so that they may become objects of our awareness and be transformed.

Hence, we begin our inquiry into the Big Assumptions with a classic mindfulness practice. Our task is to simply watch how our Big Assumptions shape our choices and actions throughout the day. As simple as it sounds, this practice is challenging. The first challenge is to actually remember the Big Assumption you want to watch in action. Since our Big Assumptions are the filters we see through, not look at, they readily slip from our attention. For this practice, I strongly recommend you write down the Big Assumption you want to attend to and keep it handy. As best you can, stay alert throughout the day for how the actions you take are grounded in your Big Assumption.

Let's say, for example, that your Big Assumption is, *If I fail in any way, disaster will befall me, and my life will crumble and be irredeemable.* You may notice that you were avoiding taking risks, even small ones. Your Big Assumption is probably at work again. It is essential in this practice to *not* judge yourself, berate yourself, or try to change your actions! Simply notice that your Big Assumption is in action again. If you can, mentally turn towards that Assumption and greet it: *Hello my old friend, I see you're still hard at work.* Do not push back against it, but acknowledge it as openheartedly as you possibly can. If possible, write down where your Big Assumption showed up in your behaviors and inspired your actions. The folks who follow through with this practice fight find it wonderfully revealing. Even brief glimpses of how a Big Assumption shapes your thoughts, decisions, and actions, whether mundane or profound, is startling.

Ongoing observation of our Big Assumptions in action often raises important questions about our free will. As we notice the power of our invisible Big Assumptions to shape our most mundane daily behaviors, it raises the question of whether we are in charge of our lives are not. This is an important question, and deserves *not* to be answered. To the degree that we can avoid deciding whether we are in charge of our daily actions are not, we permit awareness to evolve our consciousness.

Be patient with yourself. It is quite natural to avoid observing our hidden Big Assumptions in action. We would rather not look at how they preserve the world we have created and become accustomed to. In this, and all of our practices, it is essential to be gentle with yourself. It took a long time to build the mental and emotional fortifications that keep you unaware of your motivations. Attacking them too directly or forcefully will only frighten you away from the process.

<hr>

A Spiritual Frame

As Goswami's take on the New Science cosmology suggests, we are engaging non-locality. As we stand in the silent indeterminate sea of non-locality we permit something greater to transform us.

<hr>

Tools for Daily Practice

Your practice is to mindfully observe your Big Assumption(s) throughout the day whenever possible. I recommend you write your Big Assumption on a note card and keep it in your pocket or purse. Whenever necessary, look at it to remind yourself of the Big Assumption you are working on and notice how it shapes your choices throughout the day. Again, do not judge or berate yourself in any way. Simply notice!

LONG AGO AND FAR AWAY
(WRITING THE HISTORY OF OUR BIG ASSUMPTIONS)

Truths are as much a matter of questions as answers.
Ozzie Zehner

This tool is very straight forward, though it is common for individuals to avoid using it. It is, quite simply, to write the history of the Big Assumption you're exploring. Writing the history of the Big Assumption means that you follow it back as far as possible. Describe the setting and what happened. How did this or that event shape your personal Big Assumption? Describe as many instances as you can that provide *evidence* confirming the *truth* of your Big Assumption. (This will be particularly useful when we bring the work of Byron Katie to this process).

<hr />

A Spiritual Frame

Writing the history of your Big Assumption engages you in a truly divine exploration. Remember our exploration of how the world is made of stories? In important ways, the answers you get to when you examine your Big Assumptions are not important. It is the questioning that matters. As this cosmology points out, our Big Assumptions are nothing but thoughts in a whirlpool of other thoughts that confirm each other. As long as they remain invisible, every thought in our Big Assumption story confirms the next thought in the story in a swirling pile of debris that buries your intrinsic divinity. What we typically don't realize is that all of those thoughts are illusory; they are meaningless sparks off our nervous system. Again, the insight that creates freedom is the realization that these thoughts cannot withstand Inquiry. Looking at them and investigating them destroys their power. When we look at them without trying to replace them with different or better thoughts, we make a leap of faith. We trust that something beyond our limited consciousness will open us to in our interior freedom.

<hr />

Tools for Daily Practice

When you wrote the history of your Big Assumption there were likely events, or highlights, that stood out to you. You can deepen the power of your mindful observance of a Big Assumption in action by connecting it to particular events in its evolution. Two strategies suggest themselves. First, acknowledge the long history of your Big Assumption Story and the significance of the events that led you to create it. Just notice it, without judgment or internal commentary. Second, if remembering the origins of your Big Assumption Story stirs emotions, then simply allow yourself to be present to the feelings until they pass away.

Check it Out!
(Safe Tests)

"Is this some sort of test?"
"Everything that doesn't kill you is."
"Mind you," he added, "surviving doesn't
always mean you passed."
Michelle Sagara West

Iterative Safe Tests

As described in chapter 1, Kegan and Lahey use Safe Tests as a primary tool for questioning into and challenging Big Assumptions. They use the acronym SMART to frame the process:

- **S**: It's Safe.
- **M**: It's Modest.
- **A**: Actionable.
- **R**: Research.
- **T**: It's a Test.

In our small groups we work in pairs to create tests that are truly safe and modest. The goal is to create a simple test of a Big Assumption that can be carried out soon, will raise questions about the veracity of the Big Assumption, and provide important counter evidence. Let's say one of the participants, John, holds a Competing Commitment to not being told what to do. He wants to investigate an Assumption behind this Commitment. He has discovered two Big Assumptions behind this self-protective Commitment. First, he assumes if he was told what to do, his life would become drudgery; and second, that he would lose his creativity. A good Safe Test of these Assumptions would be to find someone he trusted and allow that person to give him instruction on one aspect of a minor project and see how he felt. If John has made his Safe Test sufficiently modest and safe, he will experience a positive outcome. John will notice that, even though he was told what to do, his work life did not become drudgery and he remained creative.

John's challenge, then, is to integrate this piece of information into his existing Big Assumption. The nature of a Big Assumption is that it frames our reality; it tells us what to include and what to exclude in our mental model of how the world works. Because it effectively filters the reality we see, John's Safe Test will not impact his Big Assumption unless he uses it to consciously challenge that Big Assumption. John's challenge is to notice, and acknowledge, that he allowed himself to be instructed by a colleague and that his creativity did not diminish nor did his job become drudgery. A small group can support John by insisting he take this evidence in to his awareness. If John lets this new bit of counter evidence into his Big Assumption, a revised Big Assumption might be: *I assume if I take direction from someone else that my work life will become uncreative,* except when direction is minimal and I take it from a person I like and trust. John has taken a baby step to nuance and *grow up* a Big Assumption. Additional, slightly riskier Safe Tests will slowly nudge John's Big Assumption into a closer match with reality.

Natural Safe Tests

Creating iterative Safe Tests as suggested above can be challenging. They require a level of motivation that may be absent in voluntary groups. I find a variation on these tests to be very effective and appropriate for these settings. I call them Natural Safe Tests.

Natural Safe Tests arise spontaneously throughout our day. They are the events and situations that would naturally raise doubt about the veracity of our Big Assumptions if we were able to see them better and let them in. Returning to John's example, it is quite possible that John takes instruction from other individuals throughout his day without realizing it. These may be very simple instructions or directions to do something, but they are invisible to John because they don't trigger the dire consequences of his Big Assumption. It might be something as simple as loading the copy machine. This is a real, live, Natural Safe Test of his Big Assumption that he doesn't notice.

A Spiritual Frame

According to the cosmology of Sofia Perennis, we incarnate in Flatland to deepen our souls as we open to the vagaries of material life. We are constantly presented with Natural Safe Tests to challenge the egoic stories that separate us from our divine nature. As the Gospel of Thomas suggests, as we test what troubles us, we emerge into the One. And from the Buddhist perspective, testing our stories deconstructs the illusions we live within and offers access to our intrinsic wisdom.

Tools for Daily Practice

Adapting Safe Tests in our daily life is very straight forward. With regard to our Natural Safe Tests, simply attend to the challenges to the Big Assumption Story as they arise spontaneously throughout your day and to write them down. Simply notice that, *Hmm, that event did not match the expectations of my Big Assumption, so perhaps my Big Assumption story is not as accurate as I thought.* It's important to write down these naturally arising Safe Tests before the filter of their Big Assumption obliterates them from consciousness.

You can also construct Safe Tests on the fly in your daily activities. I recommend keeping a written version of the Big Assumption you're working on with you at all times. Whenever you have an opportunity, try a *very small* Safe Test. If, for example, your Big Assumption is that people will not find you interesting unless you gossip, create a simple Safe Test: in your next (short) conversation refrain from gossiping. At the end of the conversation notice that it was still a good conversation and that you continue to be liked. Write down a slightly revised Big Assumption: *I assume that if I don't gossip, I won't have any friends to talk to, unless it's a short conversation with (say) Julie.*

THEY'RE ONLY THOUGHTS!

*I seem to have run in a great circle, and met myself
again on the starting line.*
Jeanette Winterson

This is another simple, but powerful, tool to add to our kit. It requires that we begin to notice the thoughts that lead us down the path of our Big Assumption Story. The technique is, very simply, to catch the thoughts that would typically spiral us down into our Story, and redirect them. This will feel uncomfortable and illegitimate at first. But your Big Assumption Story is a story you created in innocence at a very early age. Nonetheless, you did create it, and you have the right to change it any time you like. This is a good time. As soon as you can notice the thoughts that drag you down, change the story!

Here is a simple example. Let's say my boss got angry with me today. I'm at home in the evening and the event starts to replay in my mind.

Thought A: My boss sure was pissed at me today!

Thought B: But this isn't the first time. He's been mad at me a lot lately.

Thought C: Oh! This is bad!

Normally, Thought C would set off a cascade of thoughts in rapid succession: *My job's on the line! I'll probably get fired! Then I won't be able to make my mortgage payment! My house will get repossessed!* And on and on. Soon I'm depressed and frightened. But I can stop this line of thought simply by inserting a different train of thought:

Thought X: My brother Jake said he had a flat tire today.

Thought Y: But it was okay because a pretty lady stopped and gave him a ride.

Thought Z: I wonder if they'll start dating?

Thoughts X, Y and Z have *nothing* to do with thoughts A, B, and C. That's the point! Thoughts are just that, thoughts. It's reported that we have about 70,000 of them every day. And for the most part, you forget them right after you think them because you're off to the next important thought. This technique simply interrupts the thought streams that set off the dire expectations of your Big Assumptions and redirects them.

A Spiritual Frame

Neuropsychology, as part of the modern cosmology of neuroscience, suggests that by redirecting our thoughts we might actually rewire the brain. And, according to the Buddhist emphasis on stories, any time we disrupt the train of thoughts constructing our world of suffering, we break through their illusion to better see reality.

Tools for Daily Practice

This tool is particularly valuable throughout the day. The challenge is to catch your thoughts before they run away with you. Begin by watching the thoughts that lead you into fear, sadness, or anger. Whenever possible, quickly write down the initial sequence of thoughts that sets off one of these reactions. Try to catch one of the sequences right at the beginning and arbitrarily shift to another series of thoughts. It can be helpful to have an alternative thought sequence to dive into. If, for example, you are a football fan, you can divert your self-destructive thoughts into speculation about an upcoming game, the friends you will watch it with, and the kind of beer you will drink. Simply note the discomfort you may feel doing this, and proceed anyway!

I AIN'T GOIN' THERE!
(WRITING INTO FEAR)

If you find yourself in hell, keep going.
Winston Churchill

It's common in human life to be captured by our fears or anxieties. When we become anxious, our thoughts swirl around the anxiety, our bodies tense up; we become restless and our anxiety increases. Our natural response is to try to get rid of our anxiety or fear by pushing it away, or by hiding from it. But it doesn't work; it doesn't get rid of the fear or anxiety. At best it hides it temporarily. So, we write into our fear step by agonizing step. It is agonizing because the mind frantically struggles to divert our attention from this task. We write because the brain is no place for serious thought and writing keeps us on track. Even when we write, our brains will try to distract us from our task. If it's written, at least we can pick up where we left off when we regain focus

Let's return to John's story. John assumes that if he got bossed around by others he would lose his creativity. *I Ain't Goin' There!* invites John to sit down with that assumption and experience it fully. He is asked to imagine what it would be like if his creativity just evaporated. John then describes what he believes he would experience as thoroughly as possible *in writing*. When his mind wanders away, as it will, John returns his attention to his discomfort and anxiety. If he stays engaged and continues the process, he will experience a moment when the thoughts, and the related emotions, end. They will simply end. He can then move on to the next part of his Big Assumption story, write about it, and experience it fully.

I Aint Goin' There! or *Writing Into Fear* utilizes an ancient tool of self-awareness: the insight that every emotion or feeling has its own lifecycle. If you attempt to cut it short, you only maintain it. The shorthand is: *What you resist persists.*

I Aint Goin' There! is precisely the opposite of our previous tool: *They're Only Thoughts!* Whereas that tool redirects you away from the thoughts that would spiral you downward into your Big Assumption, this tool invites you to engage every step of your Big Assumption Story.

❧

A Spiritual Frame

I Aint Goin' There! *connects closely with the Christian liturgical year considered as a spiritual path. During Lent, Jesus must enter Jerusalem, the place of his death, and confront his deepest fears. In confronting each fear without turning away, the bottom eventually falls out. We call it Easter, or awakening. Similarly, when we confront the illusory story of self that keeps us captive, eventually we fall through into fuller awareness.*

～⦿～

Tools for Daily Practice

Fear and anxiety can arise at any time. During our waking hours we can generally distract ourselves or push them away, but not always. At night, fears can take on particular poignancy. As indicated above, taking the time to write into those fears is very powerful and, if you see it through, generally successful. Sometimes writing it down is not possible but you can still use this tool in powerfully transforming ways.

Whenever you find yourself caught up in fears or anxiety, during the day or in the middle of the night, turn your attention directly into it! This will take a concerted effort of will. The mind will do everything in its power to divert you from your fear. But the only way out of fear is through it. The mind says *if you go into this fear you will never return!* The surprising truth is precisely the opposite. If you can bring your attention fully to the fear you are feeling, it dissipates almost instantly. In my experience, it is most difficult to bring my attention directly into whatever is frightening me in the moment. But once I have been able to look at it directly, it disappears within seconds.

IS IT TRUE?
(THE WORK OF BYRON KATIE)

> *When you argue with Reality you will lose, but only*
> *100 percent of the time.*
> **Byron Katie**

Is It True? comes from the spiritual teacher Byron Katie. Katie presents a startlingly simple process with profound ramifications. The basic procedure involves four questions and three possible turnarounds. We begin with the four questions[30]:

•Is it true?
(Is it true that Jane shouldn't have yelled at me? Answer honestly. [Likely with *Yes*])

- **Can you be absolutely certain it's true?**
(Can you be absolutely certain that Jane shouldn't have yelled at you? Perhaps, Jane was having a bad day. Maybe you did something to piss her off, etc. Often the answer will be, *No, I cannot be absolutely certain that Jane shouldn't have yelled at me*. The answer may also be, *Yes*. In either case, proceed to the third question.)

- **How do you feel when you believe this thought?**
(Look deeply within. You may want to close your eyes. How do you feel?)

- **How would you feel if you couldn't believe this thought?**
(Again, look within and do your best to imagine *not* being able to have the thought, *Jane shouldn't have yelled at me.)*

TURNAROUNDS

There are three turnarounds:

- To the opposite (Jane *should have yelled at me.)*
- To the other (I shouldn't have *yelled at Jane.)*
- To yourself (I shouldn't have *yelled at myself.)*

Find three specific, genuine examples of how each turnaround is true.

In Transformational Inquiry we can apply these questions very effectively to our investigation of the Big Assumptions. In a previous exercise, folks wrote the history of their Big Assumption, with a particular focus on the *evidence* that *confirms* the truth of that assumption. We now bring that evidence under the scrutiny of the four questions and three turnarounds.

John created the following map (Figure 6.2):

COLUMN 0	COLUMN 1	COLUMN 2	COLUMN 3	COLUMN 4
COMPLAINTS OR FRUSTRATIONS (What shouldn't be)	NOBLE COMMITMENT (Improvement Goal)	DOING OR NOT DOING INSTEAD	COMPETING COMMITMENTS	BIG ASSUMPTIONS CORE BELIEFS
I really hate it when people are pushy and impatient.	I am committed to being more respectful with everyone I meet.	There are some people I just don't trust and I just won't be nice to them.	**Worry Box** I'm afraid that people will: • steamroll me • boss me, and • control my life **Competing Commitments** • I am committed to **not** being told what to do.	I assume if I am told what to do, then, • I will lose my freedom, • I will lose my creativity, • I will become a slave, and • my life will be a drudge. Then why live?

Figure 6.2 John's map for Is it True?

When John wrote the history of this Big Assumption, one piece of evidence that *confirmed* the truth of this Big Assumption was:

> When I was fifteen years old, my guidance counselor insisted that I take typing so I would have a marketable job skill. So I took typing instead of the painting class I really wanted to take. As a result, I didn't learn that I had artistic ability until much later in life, and I spent years as a drudge in an office. If he had not told me what to, my life would have been very different!

John's evidence is typical of the kinds of thoughts swirling around in our minds below our conscious awareness. The rational mind looks at this and calls it absurd. But that doesn't matter, because the rational mind never looks at it! This story, part of John's evidence, has been running and repeating itself invisibly, since he was a fifteen-year-old. It constitutes a valuable piece of evidence that, in John's mind, confirms his Big Assumption.

To apply Katie's four questions, we invite John to state the evidence as simply and directly as possible: *I was told what to do by the guidance counselor and missed my opportunity to become an artist.* We take this statement to the four questions:

Is it true?

Is it true that I missed my opportunity to become an artist because the guidance counselor insisted I take typing? John is asked not to answer too quickly, but to search inside for the answer that wants to emerge without the brain's interference. John responds with a resounding *Yes*.

Can you be absolutely certain this statement is true?

Again, John is invited to look within. Perhaps, he wonders, what if he had not gone to work in an office and had taken art classes. Maybe he would not have been that good as an artist, and the counselor's advice was actually helpful. Or, perhaps, he could have pursued his art on the side, but didn't. So in answer to the question, *Can I be absolutely certain that I missed my opportunity to become an artist because the guidance counselor insisted I take typing?* John might have to answer, *No I'm not absolutely certain.* (Most folks, when asked this question, will express some doubt and answer as John did. Others will remain certain, which is fine. They should simply continue with the process).

How do you feel when you believe this thought?

Looking within, John notices how it feels when he believes the thought: *I missed my opportunity to become an artist because the guidance counselor insisted I take typing.* He is aware that he feels angry, depressed, and frustrated. He imagines that he would've had a romantic life as an artist, traveling the world and being appreciated for his contribution. He feels cheated.

How would you feel if you couldn't believe this thought?

Closing his eyes, John imagines *not* being able to have the thought: *I missed my opportunity to become an artist because the guidance counselor insisted I take typing.* He envisions not even being able to think that thought. Like most folks, John expresses a sense of freedom and release.

JOHN'S TURNAROUNDS

Now to the turnarounds. They are: 1) to the opposite; 2) to the other; and 3) to the self. Katie would invite John to find three specific, genuine examples of how each turnaround is true. In my experience, finding three pieces of evidence for three turnarounds is seldom necessary. In fact, the process is so powerful that it does its work before you can come up with three turnarounds. The turnarounds for John's statement, *I missed my opportunity to become an artist because the guidance counselor insisted I take typing*, might go as follows:

1. **To the opposite:** I became an artist even *though the guidance counselor insisted that I take typing.* Perhaps John has had some success as an artist, though not what his childhood imagination might have hoped for. Even without a lot of commercial success, John finds painting to be a wonderful release after a hard day of work.

2. **To the other:** *I became an artist* because the counselor insisted I take typing. John recalls that he learned important skills of manual dexterity in his typing class that contributed to his art.

3. **To the self:** *I missed my opportunity to become an artist because* I insisted that I take typing. Upon reflection, John recalls that he was really afraid to explore his artistic ability. His family had little or no appreciation of art, and he felt he really should take something practical.

Again the wonderful thing about this process is that you don't really have to get all the way through it for it to work. The point is not to come up with a different answer; the point is to challenge the stressful thought. This is at the heart of Inquiry, which is never about getting a better answer. It's about questioning into the debilitating belief or assumption and allowing it to change. John cannot just stop believing that he missed his opportunity to become an artist because the guidance counselor insisted he take typing. Rather, as he questions into it, the belief is brought into the light, and awareness transforms it.

The great possibility that arises when we apply Katie's work to the Big Assumptions is that there is no limit to how far we can follow them. Every spiritual tradition points to that which is beyond the mind, and this work points in that direction. When the great Indian sage, Ramana Maharshi, was asked how one could attain enlightenment, he answered very simply, "Ask who you are, and don't stop until you know." He was not suggesting you continually repeat the question *Who am I?* Rather, he invites each of us to question deeply into the self we believe we are. In a similar manner, Katie invites us to inquire into the beliefs that construct the sense of self we are so committed to. In both cases, there is no answer to the inquiry, simply a ceasing of the question. We cease to identify with the sense of self that has directed our lives. This is not an inquiry available to, or appropriate in, business, government and educational settings in which Immunity to Change is typically used. In the faith context, however, the possibilities are not restricted.

ം⁓ംⓔ⁓ം

A Spiritual Frame

If our world is made of stories, and our stories keep us trapped in a prison of our own creation, and the way out is to question our stories, then Inquiry shows the path to inner freedom.

As Sofia Perennis claims, we are an image of the divine projected into space and time. Our journey across Flatland, our recital, is our way of helping God to make order out of chaos. As we follow our longing to return to our origin, we question the illusions that keep us trapped in duality.

ം⁓ംⓔ⁓ം

Tools for Daily Practice

The Work of Byron Katie offers extraordinarily powerful tools for everyday life. The point of applying Katie's questions and turnarounds to the Big Assumptions is not to have to walk through the process sequentially each time, but to thoroughly integrate the process so that different tools are available as needed.

The questions, Is *it true?* and *Can you be absolutely certain it's true?*, provide a powerhouse for transforming consciousness on an ongoing basis. Simply asking these questions of a disturbing thought is often sufficient to eliminate the thought. Or combining the question, Is *it true?*, with a turnaround can immediately eliminate the power that thought.

For example, a friend told me of how effectively he had use Katie's Work in a difficult divorce. His daughters had become alienated and would no longer talk to him. This was a source of great anguish for him and arose often in his mind. His thought was something like: *My daughters no longer love me.* Sorrow would overwhelm him. In response to this pain he would first ask Is *it true?* and wait. If the answer came back as *yes!*, he would use the second inquiry: *can I be absolutely certain my daughters no longer love me?* He would remember close relationship he had with his daughters, he would recall the false stories that had been propagated, and he would remember how susceptible his daughters were. His answer to the question would be *No, I can't be absolutely certain my daughters no longer love me.* And the painful thought would lose some of its power, not because he had a different answer but because statement is brought into question.

In a similar manner, this friend might go from the question *Is it true?* directly to a turnaround. Going to the first turnaround (the opposite), he would say, *My daughters* <u>do</u> *love me* and consider its veracity. He would remember examples of how close and loving they had been. Or he would turn it around to self: *I no longer love* <u>me</u>. He would notice how he continually blamed himself for things that were out of his control. Again, it was not that any of these other answers were truer, rather they served to deconstruct the original thought that caused so much pain. After all, they are just thoughts, not the Truth.

Another strategy is to pause for a moment and allow the feelings associated with believing a painful thought to wash over you. Then imagine that you could not believe this thought, and experience the relief. The opportunities to apply the questions and turnarounds are nearly endless.

chapter 7
this too shall pass

*It's also helpful to realize that this very body that we
have, that's sitting right here right now. . .with its
aches and its pleasures. . .is exactly what we need to be
fully human, fully awake, and fully alive.*
Pema Chodron

The body never lies.
Martha Graham

In recent years I have experimented with Immunity to Change in a
unique way. Rather than working with it primarily as a mental process,
I ask groups to engage the Columns somatically. What I describe in this
section can be used as a stand-alone process, or integrated into the more
cognitive approach once the basic 4-column structure is understood.
The core practice is to identify how the Competing Commitments and
Big Assumptions show up in our emotions and bodies, and then bring
them into dialogue on that level. This has opened a wonderfully different
dimension of Immunity to Change.

There are two rounds to this process. In Round 1, participants
experience each step of Immunity to Change in their bodies and with their
emotions. Round 2 engages the great spiritual truth, "This, too, shall pass."

ROUND 1: SOMATIC ITC

We begin with complaints. The insight gained in the transition from
complaints to our Noble Commitment is that we would not complain
unless we stood for something noble and important. We begin by
focusing on something that upsets us or something that shouldn't be.

We turn inward to notice the emotion that arises and allow ourselves to feel it. We then notice where the feeling is showing up in the body. At each step, we close our eyes and really enter the feeling. I encourage folks take a bodily position representing their complaint. We then share out around the circle.

Next I ask everyone to identify the value beneath their complaint, to feel the emotion associated with it, where it resides in the body, and then take a bodily position that represents that noble value. We do not talk much about the complaint or the value. Instead, folks are invited to deeply experience the bodily emotion associated with this transition. Not surprisingly, the stronger the complaint, the more important the underlying value is to the individual.

In silence, we each consider a personal change we could make that would reflect this value or Noble Commitment. Again closing our eyes (we are still in Column 1), we explore how it would feel to make this change. When folks have a deeply felt sense of their improvement goal in their body and emotions, we share briefly and move on to Column 2.

Column 2 asks, *What are you doing, or not doing, instead (of your Noble Commitment)?* That is, what behavior or actions are you taking to thwart your improvement goal and Noble Commitment? I remind everyone that we are looking for just a small realm of free choice. There are all kinds of external factors, personal history, cultural factors, social constraints, etc., that prevent us from fulfilling our Noble Commitment. But we are looking for that little realm of free will, where we can choose one action or another. If, for example, my Noble Commitment is to listen carefully to whomever I'm talking to, and I notice that I continue to cut people off in conversation, there may be many factors that are beyond my control: the situation might be rushed; I might be in a work situation that doesn't allow time for deeper conversation; I may even be struggling with a family history of impatience; but I still have a small window (perhaps just 1 percent) of freedom of choice in this particular situation. Everyone is asked to enter into an experience, emotionally and bodily, and sense how it feels to have chosen (at least to some small degree) not to live up to their valued Noble Commitment.

The blame we feel is typically accompanied by shame. Most of us want to escape these uncomfortable feelings as soon as possible. But I invite everyone to sit in the experience of blame and shame as long as possible. The point is not to indulge in one's pain, but to become acquainted with the feeling. Remember we are not creating any new feeling, but only revealing emotions that are already present but below the surface of awareness. I am also working from the premise that blame and responsibility are not bad things, even when they are experienced with shame. Rather, blame is a cause for hope, for it opens the possibility that an individual can choose differently and make changes. The camaraderie of common experience assists this deeply.

The next step is to accept forgiveness for your genuine blame. Notice where forgiveness arises in your body. Notice the emotions associated with it. How does the sense of forgiveness move through the body? Does it have a locus? I generally allow folks plenty of time to be in this experience.

After this reprieve of forgiveness, I ask folks to return to the feeling of responsibility for thwarting their Noble Commitment and experience the tension or anxiety that arises if they consider doing the opposite (we are moving into the Worry Box in Column 3). In our example, someone might feel a great deal of tension at *not* interrupting the person they're talking to. With minimal discussion, I invite participants to sit in the tension, notice its location in their bodies, and simply experience it. Remember, we have already spent a good deal of time talking about these issues; we are now experiencing them in a different way. After spending a little time in that tension or anxiety we ask, *What is the Competing Commitment associated with this anxiety?* In our example, it may be that someone is committed to having their opinion heard, *no matter what.* How does it feel to hold that commitment? Where does it show up in the body? Again, everyone is invited to close their eyes and hang out in the emotional and bodily experiences of their Competing Commitment.

Our self-protective Competing Commitments emerge directly from our Big Assumptions, and are a natural consequence of those Assumptions. So I instruct folks to imagine doing the opposite of their self-protective Competing Commitment and complete the following statement: *I assume that if I did (the opposite), then . . .* In our more cognitive journey through ITC, an individual might say something like, *If I didn't get to speak my opinion, I might never get to verbalize something that is very important to me; if I didn't get to speak my mind, people wouldn't know that I have an opinion; I might become invisible; people would disregard me; and I would disappear.* In a parallel manner, we go step-by-step through the Big Assumption Story. At each step we pause, invite individuals to identify where the emotion is showing up in their bodies and just spend a little time with it.

As in our more intellectual exploration of Immunity to Change, we developed a map of our dynamic resistance to change. But in this case, we have done it with attention to our emotions and bodily sensations. To draw our attention to the sensations, I invite folks to bring the emotions of the Big Assumptions and the self-protective Competing Commitments into dialogue with the emotions of their Noble Commitment and experience the internal battle that wages below their consciousness awareness. This is similar to psychodrama at the level of bodily emotions.

Round 2: This Too Shall Pass

Our first pass through somatic ITC is revealing in and of itself, but we can deepen the process to directly experience the ancient spiritual truth, *This too shall pass*. We may know this wisdom intellectually, but it is of little use to us until we can experience it directly in our bodies and emotions. To do this, we repeat each step described above. But this time, we endeavor to hang in with the feelings until they dissipate of their own accord. The experience is telling, but not surprising; the pleasant emotions, like experiencing our Noble Commitment or basking in forgiveness, are quite easy to stay with until they dissipate. The painful feelings of shame, anxiety, and fear are much more difficult to abide. Two profound lessons can be learned here. First, no matter how much we want them to stay, our pleasant feelings end after a relatively short time. And, second, even though we want our painful feelings to end as quickly as possible, they, too, have their own lifecycle—*but they do end*. This is important! We are typically in such a hurry to get over feeling bad, that we don't allow our feelings to finish their cycle and they get bound up in us. But if we stay with our bodily sensations and emotions, they too shall pass away. In this exercise we move past any intellectual understanding we may have of this truth, to experience its reality directly.

Again, the practice is very straightforward: engage each of the steps explained above but this time stay with each feeling until it dissipates. If you move out of the feeling before it disappears on its own, then reengage.

Remember, our working assumption is that we are not creating new emotions but revealing feelings that are already present below conscious awareness. We are engaging a great spiritual truth that I believe to be at the core of all the world's spiritual traditions. In Christianity it is in the admonition to *resist not evil:* in Buddhism it is expressed in the highly developed notion of *impermanence*. It's the idea that every thought, emotion, and feeling has its own little lifecycle that needs to be completed. If it is not allowed to complete its cycle, it remains attached to our body, mind and emotions. If we stay with it to its end, it is done.

This can be particularly important tool for gently challenging our Big Assumptions. Experiencing the emotion associated with each step of the Big Assumption and allowing it to complete itself brings an alternative experience into that Assumption. Implicit in most of our Big Assumptions is the assumption that it is *permanent*, which elicits fear (perhaps terror). In our example, the individual has the followings string of Big Assumptions: *If I don't get to speak my opinion, I might never get to verbalize something that is very important to me; if I don't get to speak my mind, people will think I don't I have an opinion; I might become invisible; people will disregard me; and I will disappear.* Each step implies permanence. The first step is explicit: *If I don't get to speak my opinion, I will never get to verbalize something that is very important to me.* The second part of the story might be more accurately stated as: *People will never know I have an opinion.* Similarly, with the next strings: I would become permanently invisible; everyone would disregard me; and I would disappear . . . forever.

When we engage each of these steps in the Big Assumption Story, and experience it until it passes away, we somatically inquire deeply into the permanence and, hence, the validity of that portion of the Story. Let's take one part of the story above and see how this would work: *People would never know I have an opinion.* When I sit with that idea, feel the emotion and where it resides in my body, and then watch it dissipate of its own accord, I *must* doubt its veracity. This is a Core Belief, which is part of my core identity. When I engage it, it frightens me, and I generally run away, implicitly proving to myself that it must be true. But when I bring myself to actually sit with that Belief, it dissipates on its own. How could it be true? If it disappears when I simply attend to it, how can it have any reality? These are simultaneously intellectual questions, bodily sensations and emotional experiences that bring a profound questioning to the Big Assumption.

☙ ❧

A Spiritual Frame

From the cosmology of Sofia Perennis, the soul's journey across Flatland is not about avoiding challenges and discomfort, it is about engaging fully whatever life brings. In engaging life fully we create the sacred stories that help God bring order out of chaos. In the language of Christianity, we continue in Lent, the journey into shadow. In this cosmology, Jesus did not resist the emotional and physical abuse he received but allowed it to transform him. The culmination of Lent (Passion or Holy Week) brings destruction of the last vestiges of his persona. Yet this to passes and is celebrated as Easter, resurrection.

When we say the world is made of stories, we are not referring solely to our mental constructions. Every story is mental, emotional and physical. Often it is our physical and emotional responses to our mental stories that "confirm" their truth: "I felt it, so it must be true!" The process of somatic ITC and the recognition that This Too Shall Pass confronts our illusory stories on the physical and emotional planes.

☙ ❧

Tools for Daily Practice

Tools for daily use coming from this process are direct, simple, and profound. The wisdom of this practice permeates the Crazy Wisdom tools of Transformational Inquiry. Very simply, attend to your bodily sensations whenever possible. If you're feeling fear, feel fear. Watch as it arises and notice that, if you do not resist it, it passes away. Also, if you are feeling happy, feel happy. Notice that it arises and, to our disappointment, passes away. This is the nature of everything, and when realized somatically, inspires great piece and equanimity.

chapter 8
the whole shebang

Unexplored paths lead to undiscovered treasures.
Constance Chuks Friday

Inquiry is fatal to certainty.
Will Durant

This chapter draws together all the practices developed in previous sections, so that you can facilitate an Inquiry group in your community. The practices are laid out as they might be used in, say, a long-term program of Transformational Inquiry. You need not use it in this manner, but the following pages will indicate how you might string classes together for the best results. Each section will indicate different ways in which I begin classes, how I follow up from the previous week, and the homework I assign for the following week. I encourage you to follow your intuition in this work and adapt all the techniques to your personal style. The easier and more playful you are with the process, the more success you will have.

WEEK 1: BEGINNING

I begin a multi-week class in Transformational Inquiry with a six-hour retreat day. During this day together, we take our time walking through the entire four-column Immunity to Change process. Not only do folks become familiar with the scaffolding of Transformational Inquiry, they simultaneously build a community of trust that serves the entire process.

It you are the leader, it is important that you be vulnerable, appropriately revealing, and playful. This is not therapy, even though it is therapeutic. Folks are always free to not participate. They must not feel coerced to go any deeper than they choose. If you are the facilitator, you must be careful not to impose your own interpretations on participants' responses. This can be challenging, because your role is to help individuals articulate their feelings and assumptions as directly and clearly as possible. I do this by consistently asking folks if my interpretations of their statements are correct.

We begin with complaints, as in *Whining Our Way into Nobility* (see chapter 4). I invite everyone to spend a few minutes quietly writing down some of their complaints and *what shouldn't be*. They then share these complaints with a partner. After a few minutes, I ask for volunteers to share their complaints with the group. I write these complaints on a flip chart, identifying each individual so we can track their story as we move forward. This is great fun, as folks, when given encouragement, will readily get into their complaints.

We move through all of the columns in a similar manner. With every column, we reflect individually, share with a partner, then share with the group. By the end of the day, we have built a cohesive group with surprisingly deep foundations for continued work. We have become vulnerable, we have shared secrets, and we have laughed together.

We now have the basic scaffolding for the Crazy Wisdom tools of Transformational Inquiry. During the following weeks, we will mindfully work our way through each the columns, developing the tools as we go.

The homework for the following week is to:

- Pay attention to your complaints. Notice whenever you judge someone, yourself or a situation. Write down as many complaints and judgments as you can.
- Notice the intensity of your complaints and see how they feel in your body. Do they arise in a particular part of your body?
- Notice the emotions that arise with different complaints. How important does the complaint seem at the moment it arises? How important does it seem five minutes later?
- Record as much as you can.
- After you have given yourself some practice noticing your complaints and judgments, shift your perspective and ask yourself about the value or commitment behind each complaint. Again write down as much as you can.
- Also, notice how your feelings change when you make this shift. What happens in your body? Record as much as possible.

Week 2: The Shift from Commitments to Behaviors

In the following pages I work through the Crazy Wisdom tools of Transformational Inquiry in a linear manner. This is strictly a convenience for the written medium. In practice, it never works out this way, so don't feel constrained by the form presented here. Please make use of the great gift you can offer: time. Move with your intuition and allow folks to explore, but not drift off into comfortable chatter. In twelve years of practice with these tools I have never been able to present all of them thoroughly. Many people will retake this class to learn new skills and techniques or deepen the ones they have already tried.

Typically, when we gather for week two, folks are eager to share their experiences and insights. Again, I invite everyone to share with a partner (it need not be the same partner). Not only do partners share their complaints and commitments, they also share their insights. Folks are often alarmed at how much they complain and judge, far more than they could ever record. The embarrassment we experience when we begin to recognize just how much we judge and complain is contained and counter-balanced by the awareness that we all do this.

As a leader, it is important to frame complaints not as problems, but as the mind doing *exactly what it is supposed to do!* Our complex minds evolved to differentiate, to weigh situations, to notice problems or dangers and consider strategies. The mind judges; it's that simple. We cannot stop it, but we can have something to say about how seriously we take the mind's judgments and complaints. It is important to spend some time on this topic. Our culture insists that complaining is bad and that we should not indulge ourselves. As a result, we either feel bad for complaining or deny that we are judging. Either strategy effectively removes complaints and judgments from our awareness. When we are not aware of them, they run our lives.

After affirming both the naturalness of complaints and their value in our lives, we explore the commitments behind our complaints, first with partners and then in the larger group. Consistently, folks comment on how their sense of themselves shifts when they turn their attention to the values behind their complaints. This insight reframes the importance of complaints; rather than seeing them as a practice to avoid, complaints become a resource for investigating important commitments that individuals hold.

A good deal of personal empowerment emerges in this first, simple step of Inquiry. Folks make a subtle, but important, shift from a negative self-image as a complainer and whiner to someone who stands for something important. This shift serves to embolden folks as they move more deeply into their hidden Commitments and Big Assumptions.

Participants are now invited to select the most important values emerging from their complaints. Using the tools outlined in in chapter 4, each person chooses a Noble Commitment or improvement goal.

At this point I often use a playful, guided meditation to clarify the Noble Commitment. Everyone is asked to stand, close their eyes, and sway gently from side to side, focusing on the feeling in their bodies. Then, asking them to keep their eyes closed, I invite them to take the pose of their Noble Commitment and experience how it feels from the inside. When they open their eyes, volunteers are asked to briefly tell, amid loving, supportive laughter, how this posture expresses their commitment. Finally, everyone takes their seats and, again closes their eyes. They are then instructed to envision how their Noble Commitments would cause them to act in the world. After a few minutes, they slowly open their eyes and share their thoughts with partners and then with the larger group.

We are now ready to move into the Column 2 question: *What do I do, or not do, to keep my Noble Commitment from being realized?* This is not about judging ourselves. We are not going to fix anything. Quite the opposite! We are on a journey of discovery and this is an essential step along the way. If we get caught up in berating ourselves or trying to change our behaviors, we miss the deep understanding we are pursuing.

As folks articulate the behaviors that thwart their Noble Commitments, we enter into our discussion of blame and forgiveness (see chapter 4). The central insight to remember is to *accept only as much blame as you can accept forgiveness.* This tends to be trickier than it sounds. So, I first invite everyone to take one of their behaviors and list all the excuses they have for that behavior.

Let's say their Noble Commitment was to be more generous, and the behavior that thwarted that aspiration was that they did not give any money to homeless persons they met on the street. Some of their excuses might be: *I was in a hurry. It was a busy intersection and I was concerned about stopping. I got yelled at today and wasn't in the mood to help anybody. My parents were stingy and I get it from them.* Then the social excuses will chime in, the ones provided free-of-charge by our culture: *Lazy bum! Go get a job! He'll just spend it on drugs and alcohol. He didn't really look needy, that was a nice coat he had on! It's probably a scam!* I insist that folks not underplay these excuses. In fact, they should err on the side of exaggeration and give themselves more excuses than blame. I then ask them to search for that area of free choice. We find this much more difficult to do because our brains will frantically try to avoid looking in the direction of blame and shame. So, if it feels painful to acknowledge some personal responsibility, you're on the right track!

I have people pair off and share both their excuses and the language of their free choice with their partner. I ask them to estimate the percentage of free choice they really had. I encourage everyone to keep this number small, under 5 percent. The listening partner not only listens but encourages, and even helps find excuses. In our sharing, we want to look at both our excuses and our free choice for acting against our Noble Commitments. It is important to share both of these with a partner as it can make accepting forgiveness easier.

Once folks have had time to share with their partners, we enter into a short, guided meditation. I ask folks to recall the freely-chosen behavior that impedes their Noble Commitments, to notice where they feel it in their bodies, and to be aware of the shame, pain and remorse likely to be associated with this choice. I don't leave them with this for very long, because the mind will run away as quickly as possible. So I ask them to imagine some force, God, the universe, a parent, or their higher self, flooding them with understanding and forgiveness. I ask them to envision opening their arms to receive that forgiveness. I then invite folks to reflect individually for a few minutes and then share with their partners. We then come together as a group to explore the challenges and results of our process.

The homework for the following week is to:

- Work with only one Noble Commitment.
- Notice and record anything you do, or avoid doing, that keeps this Commitment from being realized.
- Whenever possible, focus on one behavior. Think about, and perhaps write down, all of your excuses for that behavior. Be generous with your excuses!
- Then explore your realm of freedom. Every time you can identify personal responsibility and blame (you'll recognize it by the feeling of shame that arises immediately) immediately accept forgiveness from whatever source suits you.
- Try to notice how your body responds to each of these different practices.
- **Don't fix anything!!** Simply experience!

WEEK 3: THE SHIFT FROM BEHAVIORS TO WORRIES AND COMPETING COMMITMENTS

The group is ready to kill me when we gather next! The reason is simple: it's *really* hard to just notice our self-defeating behaviors without trying to fix them, or to not berate ourselves along the way. It's challenging to discover an appropriate degree of blame and responsibility for our actions. It can be even harder to accept forgiveness.

Upon returning to the group, we partner immediately and give folks plenty of time to share their struggles with blame and forgiveness, with the behaviors that thwart their Noble Commitments, and to share how challenging it was to *not* try to fix things. We then invite volunteers to share with the entire group. As you can imagine, the sense of common humanity, vulnerability and trust are building as we move from week to week. A good-hearted gallows humor arises from the growing understanding of how similar we are, how complex, and how wonderfully imperfect.

As you will recall, the transition to self-protective Competing Commitments is a two-step process. The first step is to consider doing the opposite of your Column 2 behaviors and notice what tension, anxiety or fear arises. The second step is to translate these into Competing Commitments. See chapter 5 for details. It will take most of a two-hour class to uncover the anxieties associated with doing the opposite of our Column 2 behavior, to translate them into good Competing Commitments, and to investigate our dynamic Immunity to Change.

Remember, it is important to state our Competing Commitments in the simplest, most childish, and perhaps most embarrassing, manner possible. The more raw the statements are, the more powerful they are. At each step of the way, folks share with a partner and then with the larger group, as they are willing. If time permits, I ask folks to reflect on where their dynamic Immunity to Change has shown up in recent activities and to share this with a partner, and finally to share with the group.

Time permitting, we may also do a short meditation. Everyone stands up with their eyes closed and sways gently back and forth. I ask them to feel a Noble Commitment and take its posture. Then I ask them to feel a Competing Commitment and take its posture. Finally, and this is really fun, I ask them to imagine their Noble and Competing Commitments in combat, and then to alternate their postures between to two . . . without whacking their neighbor.

The homework for the following week is to:

- Practice seeing yourself doing the *opposite* of the behavior that thwarted your Noble Commitment. If the tactic was to *avoid* doing something, then imagine *doing* what you were avoiding and, in both cases, observe and record the anxiety that arose. It is important to keep this strictly in your imagination at this point.
- Translate each of the fears that arise from your anxiety into a Competing Commitment and state it in the rawest, most childlike language available.

- Describe in writing the particular Immunity to Change pattern that is revealed by your reflections.
- **Don't fix anything!!**

WEEK 4: GETTING TO KNOW OUR COMPETING COMMITMENTS

Week four opens with a check-in on the homework. What did folks experience when they envisioned *not* doing their Column 2 behaviors? We break into pairs to share our experiences during the week, and then share them with the larger group. Again, we pay special attention to stating our self-protective Competing Commitments in the clearest and rawest language possible. By this point, folks are both comfortable and playful in sharing what arose for them. We spend most of this class interviewing our Noble and Competing Commitments (see chapter 5).

The homework for the following week is to:
- Write the story of your Noble and Competing Commitments.

  ◊ Use the interview questions to write the story of your Noble Commitment: *What is your name? What do you stand for? Why is this important to you? How do you try to act in the world? What are your values? Why are these important? Anything else?*

  ◊ Use the interview questions to write the story of your Competing Commitment: *What is your name? What is your role in my life? Please elaborate. Why is it important that you do this job? If you didn't do this job, what might happen? Why does this matter to you? Is there anything else you would like to share with me?*

WEEK 5: FROM COMPETING COMMITMENTS TO BIG ASSUMPTIONS

At this point in the sequence you can move into the Big Assumptions, as we will do here, or you can stay in Column 3 and engage in psychodrama (see Weeks 6 – 8).

We begin this class by pairing off and introducing our Noble and Competing Commitments to new partners. The rest of the class time is spent making the transition from our Column 3 Competing Commitments to our Big Assumptions. Even though we have done all of this in our initial, daylong exploration of Immunity to Change, stepping back into the process can reveal hidden depths of our Big Assumption Story.

Our hidden Big Assumptions emerge when we complete the statement, *I assume that if [I did the opposite of my self-protective Competing Commitment], then . . .* Once again, folks are asked to take some time alone to make the transition from their Column 3 Competing Commitments to their Big Assumptions and to follow their Big Assumption Story as far as they can by continuing to ask, *and then? . . .* Everyone shares with a partner, and then we return to the larger group with individuals volunteering to share their insights with the whole group. Most of our time is spent clarifying our Big Assumption Story. I generally have folks break into pairs and share their Story as thoroughly as possible. We then share out to the whole group.

The facilitator becomes particularly important at this point. The mind will work arduously to deflect our attention from unearthing our Big Assumption Story. It will do this by deflecting our story sideways into *how everything will work out fine.* Or we will follow a path that has uncomfortable, but not really dire, consequences. The facilitator's job is to keep everyone on track in this deeper exploration by pointing out where they seem to be avoiding looking deeply, or gently reminding them that their outcomes don't seem to be particularly dire.

As folks clarify their Big Assumptions, I insist that they write them down as clearly and concisely as possible. In my experience, most of us will forget our newly revealed Big Assumptions before we reach the exit. It's not a problem; it's just the brain doing its job.

The homework for the following week is to:

- Practice following your Big Assumptions as far down as possible and write what you discover.

- Write a history of the Big Assumption, recording its genesis as far back as you can remember. See *Long Ago And Far Away* in chapter 6.

WEEK 6—WEEK 8 (OR BEYOND):
FALLING IN LOVE AGAIN (PSYCHODRAMA)

At this point, we are ready to engage in psychodrama. I often spend several class periods taking folks through the three rounds of role-playing between the Noble and Competing Commitments (See chapter 5 for the details). Don't be surprised if you only get one, perhaps two, psychodramas in during the two-hour class. It is important to take your time and allow for a thorough debriefing after each psychodrama.

The homework for the following week is:

- Everyone is simply asked to journal their experience as a participant or an observer. Psychodrama is a powerful experience no matter what your role.

- The homework following the last psychodrama class is to:

  ◊ Review the Big Assumptions from the first class.

  ◊ Simply observe them in your everyday life (see *The Elephant's In Charge* chapter 6).

  ◊ Notice counterexamples that arise naturally (see *Check it Out! . . . Natural Safe Tests?* in chapter 6).

WEEK 9 (OR SO): CHECK IT OUT! (SAFE TESTS)

From this point on, we develop tools for inquiring into our Big Assumptions. I begin with Natural Safe Tests (see chapter 6). These are challenges to our Core Beliefs that arise naturally throughout the day but don't make it through the filters of our Big Assumption Story. In the homework following the psychodrama series, folks were asked to check out the validity of their Big Assumptions by watching for naturally-occurring Safe Tests. We begin this class by hearing what individuals observed, again in pairs, and then in the whole group. This is a good, spirited conversation with folks having a good laugh at their own foibles.

The remainder of the class is spent developing appropriate Safe Tests of the Big Assumption Story. These intentional Safe Tests actively question the validity of our Big Assumptions by creating situations that are, in Kegan and Lahey's language, SMART. That is, they are Safe, Modest, Actionable, Researchable, and actually Test the Big Assumption. Folks are asked to do two things on their own: first, to review a Big Assumption they want to work on and, second, to think about an action that would make a good Safe Test of their Assumption. Then they can pair off and share with one another the Assumption each is going to work on and the Safe Test each has devised. It is common for individuals to devise a test that they hope will obliterate their Big Assumption forever. Such a tactic, of course, inevitably backfires and ends up reinforcing the Big Assumption they want to get rid of. The role of a partner is to help the other person assess if his or her test truly meets the SMART criteria, and how this test will challenge a

Big Assumption. They then switch roles.

We come back together as a large group and hear what each individual is planning for his or her Safe Test. We help one another refine these tests, typically making them smaller and safer.

The homework for the following week is to:

- Continue to stay alert for naturally occurring Safe Tests of your Big Assumptions. Whenever possible write them down.

- Run your Safe Test! As soon as possible after running the Safe Test, write down your reactions, your anxieties, what you learned, and how it challenged your Big Assumption.

WEEK 10: THEY'RE ONLY THOUGHTS AND I AIN'T GOIN' THERE!

This class begins with members exploring, in pairs, and then in the whole group, how their Safe Tests went, and any new, Natural Safe Tests they observed during the week. As folks try out their Safe Tests, it is not unusual for them to become increasingly attuned to the myriad Natural Safe Tests that were invisible to them previously. We then follow the pattern from the previous week to devise new, and slightly more challenging, Safe Test of our Big Assumption.

If time permits, we explore two new tools: *They're Only Thoughts,* and *I Ain't Goin' There!* I caution you to introduce these tools only if you have plenty of time. One of the great gifts faith communities have to offer is the gift of time. The kind of deep transformational work we are doing takes time. It doesn't happen on a schedule. Finding a balance between taking ample time to share and keeping everyone engaged is essential. If, on the one hand, we spend too much time exploring whatever topics arise, we will drift back into comfortable old patterns and not engage challenges. If, on the other hand, we charge through these tools too quickly, we will not have time to absorb them adequately. A judicious balance between safety and challenge is the gift you, as a facilitator, can give.

Both of these tools, *They're Only Thoughts"* and *I Ain't Goin' There!* are straightforward and tremendously powerful (see chapter 6). *They're Only Thoughts* is a practice for derailing thoughts that can lead us into despair or distraction. On the surface, the practice looks like an effort to fix things, but it's actually not. We do not disrupt a train of thought in an effort to replace it with a better thought. We disrupt our train of thought solely to disrupt it. It's not about the new thought; it's about disrupting old patterns.

To introduce this practice, I invite everyone to sit quietly for a few minutes and remember a situation that made them angry, upset, or depressed. I ask them to watch the sequence of thoughts that gets them upset. This can be quite challenging. Typically a sequence of thoughts, with well-ingrained emotions, can fire off in a matter of seconds at the edge of our awareness. Before we know it, we are caught up in an internal drama. So, the first step is to pay enough attention to our habituated thought patterns to slow them down and catch them before they take us over. A good way to do this is to ask folks to write down the sequence of thoughts that led to their upset and then share with a partner. As we share in the group, we seek to identify where in the thought process we might catch ourselves. We then practice catching ourselves in our thought sequence and diverting our thinking to *any* other topic. Doing this feels profoundly illegitimate!

The nature of the human mind is such that whenever we have a thought, we believe it is *our most important thought, ever*! That is, until the next thought arises, and then, of course, *it* is *our most important thought ever!* Disrupting our *most important thought ever* is perceived as a travesty. We experience anguish when breaking off a train of thought that is deeply habituated, even when that train of thought brings pain and discomfort.

For fun, I invite a volunteer to share a train of thought that upsets them. If possible, I ask them to really dive into the thought sequence and tell us all about it. In the middle of their story, I cut them off and ask about something totally unrelated. If, for example, Susan is upset that her friend criticized her hairstyle, her thoughts might run like this: *What right does she have to criticize? Hers looks like an old broom. I hate it when . . .* I cut her off in midsentence. If she has successfully engaged in this line of thinking, she is sure to be upset with me. Hurray! I have disrupted a powerful train of thought in mid-thought. I may ask her what her plans are for the weekend; is she going on a date with her husband? And so on. Now, how important does that train of thought about her friend's criticism seem? This is generally good for a round of laughter founded in self-recognition. I encourage participants to take as much time as they need in the group to practice this tool. They're always surprised at its power.

To introduce *I Ain't Goin' There* (or *Writing into Fear*), we return to our Big Assumption Story. When we made the transition from our Column 3 Competing Commitments to the underlying Big Assumptions, we dug deeply into that story by asking *and then . . .and then . . . and then?* *I Ain't Goin' There!* is essentially the same process but with deeper engagement. Of course, the practice is not limited to the Big Assumption Story but can be applied to any anxiety or fear that grabs ahold of us.

There's not a lot to do with this practice in class beyond introducing it. It's homework material. Great topics to work with are money, health, relationships and death, as well as anything that came up in the Big Assumption Story.

The homework for the following week is to:

- Try out the new Safe Test. Continue to notice naturally-arising Safe Tests.

- Practice *They're Only Thoughts!* and *I Ain't Goin' There!* at least once each during the week.

WEEK 11: REVIEW AND RENEWAL

We have done a lot of difficult, important work! I encourage you to stop at this point, and at any other point along the way, to simply explore what you have done. I have been presenting the Crazy Wisdom tools of Transformational Inquiry as if we could do it week after week, but folks generally need more time to absorb the process. This is a good time for that.

I begin this class by inviting everyone to share the results of their latest Safe Test. After debriefing, we explore the outcomes and challenges they experienced using *They're Only Thoughts!* and *I Ain't Goin' There!*

The homework for the following week is to:

- Return to the section called *Long Ago and Far Away* (the history of your Big Assumption in chapter . . . .) and rewrite it, citing as much *evidence* as possible for why your Big Assumption is true.

WEEK 12+: IS IT TRUE?
(THE WORK OF BYRON KATIE)

The work of Byron Katie often requires several weeks of practice (see chapter 6). The great virtue of this work is that it can take an individual beyond their personal sense-of-self and offer a taste of the Infinite. By engaging the evidence for elements of the Big Assumption Story, we develop a profound set of spiritual tools that can potentially lead us into the sacred realm of not-knowing.

We apply Katie's work to the *evidence* that *proves* to the individual that their Big Assumption is true. After a brief introduction, we begin with the worksheets provided by Katie (see Appendix E). Two worksheets are included here. One is entitled *One-Belief-at-a-Time Worksheet* the other is the *Judge Your Neighbor Worksheet*. Depending upon the evidence you are inquiring into, one worksheet or the other will be appropriate. I begin by asking for a volunteer to work on an issue. I gently walk them through the four questions and the turnarounds. Now that we have an example, we can dive right into leading a partner through the four questions.

If you want to do the work of Byron Katie with your group, I strongly recommend that you first read her book, *Loving What Is*. Then listen to the audio version of this book to hear Katie in action, and then watch several of her online sessions.

WEEK 14: THIS TOO SHALL PASS

Finally, we step back into the four-column process of Immunity to Change, this time in the body (see chapter 7). You need not wait until the end to practice this powerful tool. It can be inserted at any time after you have established a caring, trusting group.

appendix a:

theoretical foundations of transformational inquiry

THE BIG PICTURE

QUADRANTS

LINES OF DEVELOPMENT

STAGES OF DEVELOPMENT

STATES OF CONSCIOUSNESS TYPES

THE THEORETICAL FOUNDATIONS OF IMMUNITY TO CHANGE

THREE PLATEAUS IN ADULT MENTAL COMPLEXITY

THE SOCIALIZED MIND

THE SELF-AUTHORING MIND

THE SELF-TRANSFORMING MIND

TECHNICAL VERSUS ADAPTIVE CHANGE

A DYNAMIC IMMUNE SYSTEM

SUBJECT/OBJECT RELATIONS

THE BIG PICTURE

The Crazy Wisdom tools of Transformational Inquiry are part of a larger visionary perspective regarding the important role faith communities can play in a dynamically changing world. That visionary perspective comes from Integral Theory. The Crazy Wisdom tools of Transformational Inquiry focus on facilitating personal evolution from one developmental stage to the next. Here I will briefly outline Integral Theory and show where Transformational Inquiry fits into this model.

The graphic above summarizes this introduction to Integral Theory. The symbol is borrowed from a new initiative called CommonHouse™ which brings together multiple perspectives dedicated to supporting the evolution of human consciousness and is guided by the integral map. The flower in the center represents these multiple perspectives. When replaced by a cross, it symbolizes an integral Christian church, dedicated to celebrating the full depth of Christianity through the integrated perspectives of God as self, other, and structure.

Integral Theory offers a comprehensive map of reality built around five core categories: Quadrants, Lines of Development, Stages of Development, States of Consciousness, and Types.

QUADRANTS

The graphic below describes the four-part circle behind the flower. As represented by Ken Wilber, the Quadrants represent four non-reducible, interrelated perspectives that encapsulate human existence.

The **Upper Left Quadrant** represents the perspective from the interior of the individual. *What do I see when I look through my eyes, feel with my emotions, perceive with my mind?* This is the perspective from the *inside* of the *individual*, the *I* or *me*.

- The **Lower Left Quadrant** indicates the perspective from the interior of the collective. *What do I experience when I hang out with my friends and we feel like we really understand each other?* This is the *inside* of the *collective*, the *We* or *Culture*.

- The **Upper Right Quadrant** highlights the perspective from the exterior of the individual. *When I look at you, what do I see? When I look at you or anything from an objective perspective, what kind of it do I see?* This is the *outside* of the *individual*.

- The **Lower Right Quadrant** represents the exterior of the collective. *How do all the things I see or understand fit together?* This is the *outside* of the *collective*, the *its*, or how do all of the *its* fit together?

These questions and their associated fields of study are summarized below:

	INTERIOR/SUBJECTIVE	**EXTERIOR/OBJECTIVE**
INDIVIDUAL/ONE	Interior of the Individual Self and Consciousness Intention "I" • Who am I? • What is it like to be me? Studied by: • Psychology • Spirituality • Phenomenology **UPPER LEFT**	Exterior of the Individual Behavior Brain and Organism "IT" • What are you? • What do I observe? Studied by: • Behavioral psychology • Empirical sciences • Physics, chemistry, biology **UPPER RIGHT**
COLLECTIVE/MANY	Interior of the Collective Culture and Worldview "THOU/WE" • Who am we? • What is meaningful to us? Studied by: • Cultural anthropology • Epistemology • Law/Ethics/Morality **LOWER LEFT**	Exterior of the Collective Social System and Environment "ITS" • How do the "its" fit together? Studied by: • Systems theory • Economics • Sociology • Politics **LOWER RIGHT**

Figure A.1: The Quandrants

LINES OF DEVELOPMENT

Lines of Development illuminate the immense complexity of humans. Howard Gardner labels these diverse Lines of Development "multiple intelligences." They include the mental, emotional, musical, moral, aesthetic, interpersonal Lines of Development (somewhere between one and two dozen lines have been identified). Our different intelligences, however, are not equally developed in all of us. As we know, we are all better at some things than we are at others. We may excel at mathematics yet, at the same time, be terrible at interpersonal relationships; or we might be athletic on the one hand, but get lost walking around the block. It is the job of the *self-line* to weave all of these intelligences into a more or less coherent sense of *me*. We call it ego.

When we speak of *personal development* we are speaking of the developmental trajectory of the self-line through distinct, qualitatively different stages (see the next section). The personal lines of development are most relevant to the tools developed in this book. But each Quadrant is comprised of a variety of quasi-independent Lines at different stages of development. The Lower Left Quadrant includes developmental sequences of morality, ethics, and worldviews; the Upper Right Quadrant includes such diverse Lines as language, physiology, and stars; while the Lower Right contains such Lines as economics, politics, and law.

STAGES OF DEVELOPMENT

As we will use them here, Stages of Development represent the milestones of growth and development of our sense of self, the ego. Stages of Development are enduring acquisitions represented by the spiral in the background of our graphic. Each stage creates the foundation for the next stage, like a rung of a ladder. Stepping up a rung demands that we leave the previous rung. Yet we cannot abandon or destroy the previous rung as it provides the structure for the current rung. In the language of Integral Theory, each stage must *transcend and include* the previous stage if there is to be healthy development.

The Stages of Development are given different names by different theorists. Though not shown on the graphic, eight Stages of Development are part of this model[35] beginning at the bottom and becoming more inclusive as you move up the spiral. The most primitive level of our human development, Archaic, refers to our infancy. We don't really have a sense of self in infancy so it is more of a pre-Stage. The next, Magic, points to the fantastical world inhabited by children between the ages of two and six. It is a world of imaginary creatures and wonder. Following Magic, the Warrior stage emerges in middle childhood, around ages seven through twelve in contemporary Western culture. For Warrior consciousness, life is a zero-sum game: there are only winners and losers, and the goal is to gain power over others. The Warrior expresses him- or herself forcefully and *to hell with anyone else*.

The Conformist Stage emerges from the Warrior Stage in early adolescence when teens realize that, not only are they looking at others, but that others are looking at them. Self-identity, at this developmental Stage, is defined by one's relationship to the group. This may include peers, family, race or ethnicity, nation or sexual orientation. For this reason, Conformist consciousness is intensely ethnocentric, as in *my group, right or wrong*. This wave of development relies upon legitimate, external authority. This might be a priest or minister, a teacher, a book, a rock-star or fashion model. As I will describe in the following section, this Stage of Development corresponds with Kegan's Socialized Mind.

The next Stage of Development, Achiever, typically shows up in late adolescence and is generally considered the destination for adulthood in Western culture. This is Kegan's Self–transforming Mind. The individual inhabiting this developmental Stage strives to better him- or herself, to live well and improve society (see the Modern Story in Chapter 1). Whereas Conformist consciousness sees itself primarily in relationship to others, Achiever consciousness can stand outside these relationships and reflect upon them. This capacity to objectively stand outside the system is the foundation of science. Hypothetical-deductive reasoning allows evaluation of different perspectives and the possibility of choosing the *one best answer*.

I call the next stage Pluralist. This stage reached critical mass in the U.S. during the 1960s as the limitations of modernity, science and capitalism entered the public awareness. Popular confidence in technology dwindled as people noticed that science could not solve all their problems or make them happy. We became acutely aware of exploitation, the corruption of existing hierarchies, environmental degradation, the shallowness of materialism and the suffering of others. Marginalized groups, especially people of color and women, were recognized and given a greater voice. The Pluralist Stage represents the beginning of Kegan's Self-Transforming Mind, which also encompasses the next rung of development, Self-Actualization.

Self-Actualization, the next step on the developmental ladder, not only deals with paradox and ambiguity, but actually sees them as sources of inspiration. The Self-Actualized self is actively reflective in the face of complexity, change and multiple time horizons (such as past, present, near future, distant future). This reflective action involves self-guided education across different modes of learning (mental, emotional, and kinesthetic, for example), feedback from different sources, and deep attention to inner workings. This is the first stage that fully appreciates, and integrates, the contributions of the previous levels. It is the highest Stage of Development available to the ego self. Subsequent stages begin the deconstruction of the self.

The individual at the next Stage, Construct-Aware, comes to physically, mentally, and emotionally *grok* (that is, to understand profoundly and intuitively) that all objects are human-made constructs. The ego, space, and even time are seen to be based upon layers and layers of symbolic abstraction that become increasingly transparent to Construct-Awareness. The quest becomes to uncover the limits of the rational mind and *unlearn* the automatic, conditioned responses that are based on memory, everyday cultural reinforcement, even language.

The final stage is the Transpersonal wave of development[36]. This is something of a catchall phrase for several Stages of Development beyond Construct-Awareness. The successful deconstruction of the sense of a separate self (in the previous stage) opens the door to several levels of transpersonal awareness. That is, awareness beyond identification with ego.

STATES OF CONSCIOUSNESS

The fourth component of the Integral map, States of Consciousness, refers to the transient experiences that are part of everyday life. States of Consciousness are contained within the Upper Left Quadrant, the interior experience of the individual. States become more expansive as we move up the ladder from Gross to Subtle to Causal to Witnessing to Non-Dual consciousness.

The *Gross* State of Consciousness refers to the bodily sensations received through our five senses. A feeling in my stomach tells me I am hungry. A pin prick causes me pain. Wonderful tastes give me pleasure. Loud noises drive me away. All of these are states arising at the *Gross* level.

The *Subtle* State of Consciousness takes us into the mental realm. If I think about what I want to eat to relieve my hunger, or how I want to hit the guy who stuck me with the pin, or how what I am tasting reminds me of my mother's cooking, I am in *Subtle consciousness*. When I dream, I enter the purest form of Subtle consciousness as my body drops completely from my awareness and I live in a world created by my mind.

Causal Consciousness moves beyond thought. Most of us are so engaged with the chatter of our minds and our bodily sensations that we seldom notice the realm of silence beyond thinking. Silence is the *sound* of the Causal State of Consciousness

If you hang out in the silence between and beyond thoughts (Causal consciousness), you might notice that you are hanging out in silence. This is not a thought about the silence, it is a very simple awareness that you are not thinking. If you have a thought about the silence, it can take you back into subtle consciousness or you can simply notice the thought. When you simply notice your thoughts, and your body sensations, in the silence between thoughts without being absorbed in them you are in the *Witness* State of Consciousness. You simply notice that you are silent, or thinking or feeling, without any judgment or opinion. It is as if a totally impartial observer is watching all that goes on within you.

Gross, Subtle, Causal, and Witness consciousness all exist within the world of duality; there is an observer and something being observed. In *Non-dual Awareness* all distinction between observer and observed disappears. You are one with all that surrounds you. There is simply no distinction.

The salient feature of these states is that they are temporary. States of bliss, anxiety, clarity, or various altered states come and then depart. On a daily basis, we may experience moments of silence and peace (Causal consciousness), or narrowed perceptions induced by fear or anxiety (Gross consciousness), or a semi-dream state filled with wonderful insights (Subtle consciousness). All of these provide lenses through which we engage the world for a while . . . and then they change. Such are the many States of Consciousness.

TYPES

Types refer to *horizontal* differences that occur at each Stage of Development. A popular typology is the Meyers-Briggs Type Indicator, which categorizes personality types according to feelings, thinking, sensing and intuition. Another popular typology, The Enneagram, offers a similar exposition across nine types of personalities. Your personality type will manifest differently at different Stages of Development. Other types include race, gender, social class, sexual orientation and ethnicity.

In this simple map of Integral theory, the Crazy Wisdom tools of Transformational Inquiry are largely concentrated in the Upper Left Quadrant. As such, they are a subset of a larger vision of faith communities leading the evolution of human consciousness.[37] These tools are designed to carry individuals from one Stage of Consciousness to the next, as developed more fully in the next section.

THE THEORETICAL FOUNDATIONS OF IMMUNITY TO CHANGE

Over the past twenty five years, Robert Kegan and Lisa Lahey have articulated a powerful theoretical framework and created techniques to help individuals develop the mental and emotional complexity required for life in the 21st century. Transformational Inquiry builds from their theoretical framework and develops a variety of tools for communities engaging questions of meaning and ultimate concern.

In the introduction to their book, *Immunity to Change: How to Overcome It and Unlock the Potential in Yourself and Your Organization*, Kegan and Lahey articulate the critical question successful leaders in the 21st century must ask: *What can I do to make my setting the most fertile ground in the world for the growth of talent?*[38] An analogous question must be asked by faith leaders in the 21st century: *What can we do to make our communities the most fertile ground for the development of expansive understanding, inclusive compassion, and intimacy with Spirit?* The following pages summarize the theoretical foundations of Immunity to Change, the process that scaffolds the Crazy Wisdom tools of Transformational Inquiry.

THREE PLATEAUS IN ADULT MENTAL COMPLEXITY

We begin with an exploration of what it means to *develop greater mental complexity*. Let me stress from the beginning that *mental complexity* is not confined to thinking, but deeply involves the emotions as well; both head and heart are engaged. Kegan and Lahey focus on three plateaus of development most prevalent in the adult life of Western cultures: the Socialized Mind, the Self-Authoring Mind, and the Self-Transforming Mind.

THE SOCIALIZED MIND

The "Socialized Mind" is roughly equivalent to what I called Conformist consciousness. The individual organizing his or her world through the lens of a Socialized Mind is typically a team player, a faithful follower, and a reliable worker. He or she generally relies upon, and seeks direction from, the recognized leader of an organization, institution, or family. The socialized individual actively seeks to align his or her activities with the needs and goals of the group, as articulated by the recognized leader. The profound desire of individuals to fit in motivates them to focus on what they believe others want to hear. Also referred to as the *rule/role mind*, a Socialized individual finds his or her place in society by internalizing the rules of that society and playing an appropriate role.

THE SELF-AUTHORING MIND

In contrast, individuals organizing their world through the lens of the Self-Authoring Mind follow their own compass. They tend to be independent problem-solvers inspired by their own agenda. While the Socialized Mind is intently focused on personal relationships, or schools of thought, the Self-Authoring Mind can step back enough from the social environment to construct its own personal authority that evaluates and makes its own choices. A splendid analogy illuminates the difference between the Socialized and Self-Authoring Minds: "Mental complexity strongly influences whether my information-sending is oriented toward getting behind the wheel in order to drive (the Self-Authoring Mind) or getting myself included in the car so I can be driven (the Socialized Mind)."[39]

Generally speaking, the Self-Authoring Mind is the desired destination for development in Western culture; it's what we call adulthood. It corresponds to what I called the Achiever Stage of Development in the previous section.

THE SELF-TRANSFORMING MIND

An individual organizing his or her world through a Self-Transforming Mind tends to be a meta-leader. He or she is capable of standing in contradictions and holding those contradictions in a multifaceted context. Self-Transforming leaders *lead to learn*, they are *inter*dependent and *problem finding*; that is, they are on the lookout for the new issues that will arise in a dynamic, changing world. An individual organizing their world through the Self-Transforming Mind can step back from, and reflect upon, the limits of their own ideology or personal authority. In other words, "In contrast [to the Self-Authoring Mind], the Self-Transforming Mind . . . has a filter, but is not fused with it. The Self-Transforming Mind can stand back from its own filter and look *at* it not just *through* it."[40]

The Self-Transforming Mind can see that any system or plan is in some way partial or incomplete. "Therefore, when communicating, people with Self-Transforming Minds are not only advancing their agenda and design. They are also making space for the modification or expansion of their agenda or design."[41] This individual recognizes that the world is constantly changing and in motion. So they are ready to remake the map or reset their direction in response to changing circumstances. Kegan's Self-Transforming Mind combines the Pluralist and Self-Actualizing waves of development.

In a rapidly-changing world constantly presenting us with unexpected problems and opportunities, the capacity to look at a broader expanse and have fewer blind spots is clearly desirable. In faith communities this means developing our capacity to integrate more perspectives into our faith story (mental complexity); to expand our compassionate embrace to include more people, different life forms, and the earth itself (emotional complexity); to differentiate ourselves more clearly from the thoughts and stories that run through our minds; and to open our awareness to the immensity at the core of our being (spiritual simplicity). When our mental, emotional, and spiritual complexity lag behind the needs and demands of our society, we are in over our heads. We become frightened, and defensive. We are less resilient.

TECHNICAL VERSUS ADAPTIVE CHANGE

A core distinction for this work is between *technical change* and *adaptive* change. *Technical* change refers to adaptations that can be dealt with by utilizing a *well-known set of skills*. Technical skills are important: "learning how to remove an inflamed appendix or how to land an airplane with a stuck nose wheel are examples of largely technical challenges, and their accomplishment is certainly important to the patient on the surgeon's table or the nervous passengers contemplating a crash landing."[42]

In contrast, *adaptive* challenges "can only be met by transforming your mindset, by advancing to a more sophisticated stage of mental development."[43] According to leadership guru Ronald Heifetz, "the biggest error leaders make is when they apply technical means to solve adaptive challenges."[44]

A DYNAMIC IMMUNE SYSTEM

Kegan and Lahey use the metaphor of a *dynamic immune system* to depict the core of their work. "At the simplest level, any particular expression of the Immunity to Change provides us [with] a picture of how we are systematically working against the very goal we genuinely want to achieve." But more than that, the dynamic equilibrium created by our mental and emotional immune system is "preventing much more than progress on a single goal. It is maintaining a given place on the continuum of mental complexity."[45]

This dynamic immune system is not a fault in our makeup. Rather "every immune system is an intelligent force that seeks to protect you, even save your life."[46] The adaptations of our immune system "grab us at the limits of our mindsets."[47] And our mindsets always tell us about what we are thinking or feeling.

In decades of working with individuals, Kegan and Lahey have developed a deep respect for human courage. "Courage involves the ability to take action and carry on even when we are afraid."[48] Most of us deal constantly with fear. "Anxiety, we have gradually come to appreciate, is the most important—and least understood—private emotion in public life . . . [Immunity to Change] offers a schematic representation of the way a person is handling not an acute or episodic anxiety, but a *constant, if unrecognized, anxiety running continuously through his or her life*."[49]

Most of us deal successfully with our anxiety because we have developed anxiety-management systems that serve us well. These systems come at a cost, however. "Inevitably, they create blind spots, preventing new learning and constantly constraining action in some aspects of our living. These costs show up when we are unable to deliver on some genuinely desired change, the realization of which would bring us to a new, higher level of functioning in ways we truly want to attain."[50] Though we may try our best to make the changes we want to make, we often find ourselves frustrated. It's not that we lack self-will or a true desire to change. The issue is that we don't recognize the bigger dynamics at play in making the changes we desire. The question becomes, *How can we overcome our well-established Immunity to Change?*

We begin with a couple of foundational insights. First, we do not have to eliminate our entire anxiety-management system to overcome our Immunity to Change. We will always need some kind of anxiety-management system. Instead, we can learn to build a bigger, more complicated immune system that permits us to change the things we want to change. Second, it's not change that brings us anxiety; it's the feeling that we are defenseless in the presence of what we see as danger. "Overturning our Immunity to Change always raises the specter of leaving us exposed to such dangers. *We build an immune system to save our lives*. We are not going to readily surrender such a critical protection."[51] But we can *expand* an overly restrictive immune system so it will allow us to make deeply desired changes in our lives. The question is, *How?*[52]

Subject/Object Relations

At the root of Kegan and Lahey's revolutionary work is what they call *subject/object relations*. This is an abstract way of saying that the things in us that we can't see (that are *subject* to us) tend to run us, while the things that we can look at (that are *objects* of us) are things we can alter. Hence,

A way of knowing becomes more complex when it is able to *look at* what before it can only *look through*. In other words our way of knowing becomes more complex when we create a bigger system that incorporates and expands on our previous system. This means that if we want to increase mental complexity, we need to move aspects of our meaning-making from subject to object, to alter our mindset so that a way of knowing or making sense becomes a kind of "tool" that *we have* (and can control or use) rather than something that *has us* (and therefore controls and uses us).[53]

As mental capacity expands, more and more of our internal filters are brought into awareness where they can be acted upon. The plateaus of adult development described above can be characterized by what is *object* and what is still *subject* for an individual.

Individuals looking through (or *subject* to) the Socialized Mind will be highly attentive to their immediate relationships. These may include their families of origin, religious or political affiliations, leaders in the work setting, or close friends. Anxiety and fear are focused on being cut out, or excluded, from the family or faith group, or receiving the disfavor of a work leader.

At the next level of complexity, the Self-Authoring Mind, the individual can distinguish the opinion of others from their own opinion (make it an *object* for consideration). He or she will take the opinion of others into account but can choose how much to include and how those others might influence his or her choices. Unlike folks operating through a Socialized Mind, individuals perceiving through a Self-Authoring Mind can see the opinions of others as *objects* they can accept or not.

Perceiving through the Self-Authoring Mind does not release one from anxiety; it only changes the nature of the fear. When a person is no longer afraid of being excluded from their tribe, they will likely have some anxiety about falling short of their own standards, of losing control, or being unable to realize their goals.

Looking through the lens of the Self-Authoring Mind, the individual will find his or her own self-authorship to be an *object* for their consideration. The theory, ideology, or perspective that guided their agenda in the Self-Authoring Mind now becomes an object for consideration and will be held lightly. This allows the individual to explore the limitations of the framework they use to guide their actions and hold that framework tentatively and experimentally.

Developing through these three qualitatively different levels of complexity requires disturbing the comfortable balance we have attained in learning to *look at* what before we were *looking through*. This begs the question: what motivates the development of a new level of mental complexity?

To reiterate, when Kegan and Lahey speak of *increasing mental complexity* they are not referring simply to thinking processes. Instead, growing our mental complexity draws on head and heart, on thinking and feeling. That which motivates the development of mental complexity is, in their words, *optimal conflict*. By optimal conflict they mean:

- The *persistent* experience of some frustration, dilemma, life puzzle, quandary or personal problem that is . . .

- Perfectly designed to cause us to *feel the limits* of our current way of knowing . . .

- In some sphere of our living that we *care about*, with . . .

- *Sufficient supports* so that we are neither overwhelmed by the conflict nor are we able to escape or diffuse it.[54]

We all find ourselves in conflicted situations at one time or another. These situations may or may not provide optimal settings for increasing the complexity of our mental and emotional lives. The last point–that there be sufficient support so we are neither overwhelmed nor able to escape the conflict–is critical. Using the Crazy Wisdom tools of Transformational Inquiry in an expansive faith setting can create just such a context of optimal conflict. In a small group of individuals who already know one another, we invite people into a persistent dilemma that challenges their current way of knowing. In this setting folks investigate the mental and emotional structures that perpetuate their Immunity to Change, and with gentle encouragement expand those self-limiting structures.

appendix b:
summary of tools

DON'T FIX IT!

WHINING OUR WAY INTO NOBILITY (DISCOVERING A NOBLE COMMITMENT)

DAMN! NOT AGAIN! (UNDERMINING BEHAVIORS)

I REALLY DID MEAN TO HURT YOU (ACCEPTING JUST THE RIGHT AMOUNT OF RESPONSIBILITY)

WHAT, ME WORRY? (LIBERATING ANXIETIES) AND WHERE DID YOU COME FROM? (UNCOVERING OUR COMPETING COMMITMENTS)

GETTING TO KNOW YOU (INTERVIEWING OUR COMPETING COMMITMENTS)

FALLING IN LOVE AGAIN (THE PRACTICE OF PSYCHODRAMA)

DIVING IN! (UNCOVERING BIG ASSUMPTIONS)

THE ELEPHANT'S IN CHARGE (OUR BIG ASSUMPTIONS IN ACTION)

LONG AGO AND FAR AWAY (WRITING THE HISTORY OF OUR BIG ASSUMPTIONS)

CHECK IT OUT! (SAFE TESTS)

THEY'RE ONLY THOUGHTS!

I AIN'T GOIN' THERE! (WRITING INTO FEAR)

IS IT TRUE? (THE WORK OF BYRON KATIE)

SOMATIC ITC

The following is a summary of the Crazy Wisdom tools of Transformational Inquiry as developed in chapters 4 through 7. They are stated very simply in the hope that you will practice as many of them as you can, and turn them into habits.

DON'T FIX IT!

The foundational attitude grounding all the tools developed above is Don't Fix It! Stay curious and open. When in doubt, keep doubting. If you are uncomfortable, stay uncomfortable. Listen and notice what arises. If you don't try to fix life, life will fix you. Stand in the paradox and let it transform you. That's Crazy Wisdom.

WHINING OUR WAY INTO NOBILITY
(DISCOVERING A NOBLE COMMITMENT)

As a daily practice, when you notice yourself complaining or judging ask yourself, *What value do I hold that leads me to complain?* Then allow yourself to absorb the resulting self-perception.

DAMN! NOT AGAIN!
(UNDERMINING BEHAVIORS)

Your daily practice is to notice any behaviors that impede realization of your Noble Commitment. Simply observe them or acknowledge them with a non-judgmental *Ah, I did it again* and smile.

I REALLY DID MEAN TO HURT YOU
(ACCEPTING JUST THE RIGHT
AMOUNT OF RESPONSIBILITY)

As a daily practice, simply notice when you screw up. First, acknowledge that you fell short of your expectations. Then give yourself lots of excuses. But be sure to find some area in which you could have chosen differently and you didn't. Open yourself and accept forgiveness for your bad choice. Then move on.

What, Me Worry? (Liberating Anxieties) and Where Did You Come From? (Uncovering our Competing Commitments)

Whenever you can notice an activity that stymies your Noble Commitment, imagine doing the opposite and simply notice what anxieties arise for you. Do not criticize or berate yourself, just allow yourself to sit in the anxiety, to feel it, and to observe how it arises and then falls away. Then ask yourself, *What else might I also be committed to?* and see what arises within you. Finally, watch the push and pull of your dynamic immune system. Notice its patterns and power and how it keeps you stuck in particular habits. As always, don't judge or fix anything. Just smile at what you see, embrace it, and love it if you can.

Getting to Know You (Interviewing Our Competing Commitments)

Whenever you notice a Competing Commitment in action, briefly interview it. Ask it what it is protecting you from and why it is important. Do not judge or argue with the answer you receive. Simply thank your self-protective Competing Commitment and move on.

Falling In Love Again (The Practice of Psychodrama)

When your noble aspirations are frustrated by your self-protective Commitments, get pissed! Yell at them (not in public, they'll put you away). Vent your frustrations. When you get it all out, take the role of the Competing Commitment and explain your actions.

Returning to the Noble Commitment, imagine embracing your Competing Commitment as you would a frightened child. Hear what he or she is saying to you. Acknowledge the fear and the genuine desire to protect you. Listen and hold him or her in unconditional love.

Diving in! (Uncovering Big Assumptions)

When you notice you are avoiding a particular action simply ask *What must I be assuming about the consequences of this action?* and listen.

The Elephant's in Charge
(Our Big Assumptions in Action)

Simply observe your Big Assumption(s) throughout the day whenever possible. Simply notice and welcome it (them) with a smile.

Long Ago and Far Away
(Writing the History of our Big Assumptions)

Deepen your mindful observation of a Big Assumption in action by connecting it to a particular event or events in its evolution. First, acknowledge the significance of the events that led you to create it. Second, if remembering the origins of your Big Assumption Story stirs emotions, simply allow yourself to be present to the feelings until they pass away.

Check it Out!
(Safe Tests)

Attend to daily events that challenge the veracity of your Big Assumptions. Notice that some event did not match the expectations of your Big Assumption, so maybe that Assumption isn't as accurate as you thought. You can also practice devising *really* Safe Tests and trying them out on the fly. Be sure to restate your Big Assumption to integrate the new information.

They're Only Thoughts!

This tool can be particularly valuable throughout the day. Catch a debilitating train of thoughts before they run away with you. Try to catch a sequence right at the beginning and arbitrarily shift to another series of thoughts. Notice how uncomfortable this makes you feel, and proceed anyway!

I Ain't Goin' There!
(Writing into Fear)

Whenever you find yourself caught up in fear or anxiety, turn your attention directly into it! Focus your attention on the fear as directly as you can, even though your mind is doing everything in its power to divert you. Simply hang in there until the fear dissolves. Generally, one second of direct attention is sufficient; the challenge is to focus get your attention that long!

IS IT TRUE?
(THE WORK OF BYRON KATIE)

When some aspect of you Big Assumption Story grabs you, simply ask *Is it true? Am I absolutely certain it's true?* Keep asking this of every Big Assumption thought that arises. Or take the thought and turn it around to the opposite, the other or the self, and give yourself at least one example of why the turnaround is true.

SOMATIC ITC

Whenever possible, attend to your bodily sensations. If you're feeling fear, feel fear. Watch as it arises and notice that, if you do not resist it, it passes away. Also, if you are feeling happy, feel happy. Notice that the feeling arises and, to our disappointment, also passes away.

appendix c:

examples of completed four-column worksheets

EXAMPLE 1. ON BECOMING SEXUALLY ATTRACTIVE

EXAMPLE 2. ON BEING IGNORED

EXAMPLE 3. ON BEING RIGHT

EXAMPLE 4. ON WEIGHT LOSS

EXAMPLE 5. ON BECOMING A MORE CONFIDENT PRESENTER

EXAMPLE 6. ON NOT BEING IN CONTROL

This Appendix includes seven examples of completed four and five column worksheets pertaining to different topics. My purpose is to give you the flavor of actual worksheets and their diversity.

EXAMPLE 1. ON BECOMING SEXUALLY ATTRACTIVE

COLUMN 1	COLUMN 2	COLUMN 3	COLUMN 4
NOBLE COMMITMENT (Improvement Goal)	DOING OR NOT DOING INSTEAD	COMPETING COMMITMENTS (2 Steps)	BIG ASSUMPTIONS CORE BELIEFS
I would like to care for my physical being, promote my health and strength through daily exercise and healthy eating.	Instead I . . . procrastinate, sleep in, play computer games, and reward myself with food.	***Worry Box*** • If I stop doing these things and lost weight I would become sexually attractive and vulnerable. • I would become vain and self-centered **Competing Commitments** Not being sexually attractive. Not being vulnerable or losing control.	• I assume that if I was sexually attractive then . . . • lots of men would seek me out, • I would be unfaithful to my husband, • my husband would leave me, and • I would lose my job and my life would crumble.

EXAMPLE 2. ON BEING IGNORED

COLUMN 0	COLUMN 1	COLUMN 2	COLUMN 3	COLUMN 4
COMPLAINTS OR FRUSTRATIONS (What shouldn't be)	NOBLE COMMITMENT (Improvement Goal)	DOING OR NOT DOING INSTEAD	COMPETING COMMITMENTS	BIG ASSUMPTIONS CORE BELIEFS
Economic injustice Criminal injustice Domestic violence and sexual abuse lack of access to education	I am committed to seeking greater justice in speaking out against domestic and sexual violence.	Instead of speaking out . . . I keep quiet I avoid the issues I work a lot I choose hobbies that isolate me	**Worry Box** If I spoke out . . . • People would judge me and laugh at me. • People would get angry with me. **Competing Commitments** I may also be committed to . . . Being liked and respected. Not looking foolish. Not being ignored.	I assume if I ignored then . . . • I would become invisible • no one would like me, respect me or love me, • no one would hear me, • I would have to watch more families be torn apart and destroyed by sexual violence that I could have prevented, • I would be utter failure, and • my life would be worthless.

Example 3. On Being Right

COLUMN 0	COLUMN 1	COLUMN 2	COLUMN 3	COLUMN 4
COMPLAINTS OR FRUSTRATIONS (What shouldn't be)	NOBLE COMMITMENT (Improvement Goal)	DOING OR NOT DOING INSTEAD	COMPETING COMMITMENTS	BIG ASSUMPTIONS CORE BELIEFS
Elders shouldn't be duped and believing their life doesn't matter. They should be respected. They should matter to themselves and to others.	I am committed to being a real person and doing my own soul will work. I am committed to value myself and being of value.	Instead of doing my own personal work, I . . . spend my time taking care of others manage a board, help others develop their careers, go to too many meetings. take over jobs that others should be doing.	**Worry Box** I won't look like I'm doing my job. People won't like me. The real me won't be good enough. **Competing Commitments** I may also be committed to . . . being in control being admired being the center of attention.	I assume if I was not in control . . . • Everything would fall apart. • I would know what to do with myself. • I would not appear to be competent and would be relegated to mowing lawns. • I would not feel valued. • I would isolate myself and drink too much, and • my life would crumble and I would be an immense pain and sorrow.

Example 4. On Weight Loss

COLUMN 1	COLUMN 2	COLUMN 3	COLUMN 4
NOBLE COMMITMENT (Improvement Goal)	DOING OR NOT DOING INSTEAD	COMPETING COMMITMENTS	BIG ASSUMPTIONS CORE BELIEFS
I am committed to keeping off the weight I've lost.	Instead, I continue to eat large portions. I eat sugary treats. I eat too fast and eat way too much before my body feels full. I won't get enough food. I feel deprived of really important pleasure.	**Worry Box** I won't get enough food. I feel deprived of a really important pleasure. **Competing Commitments** I may also be committed to . . . Not feeling deprived in any way. Not giving up anything.	I assume that if I felt deprived then . . . • I would be consumed by desire for food. • I would be hungry all the time. • I would be in constant anguish and craving. • It would be so miserable I would rather die.

EXAMPLE 5. ON BECOMING A MORE CONFIDENT PRESENTER

COLUMN 1	COLUMN 2	COLUMN 3	COLUMN 4
NOBLE COMMITMENT (Improvement Goal)	DOING OR NOT DOING INSTEAD	COMPETING COMMITMENTS	BIG ASSUMPTIONS CORE BELIEFS
I am committed to: being more confident in my presentations, being myself and fully present in my presentations, and improving follow-through.	Instead . . . I busy myself with other things, criticize myself, procrastinate, and don't research thoroughly enough.	***Worry Box*** It will be too much and I'll be overwhelmed. I won't be able to do it well enough. Other stuff won't get done. **Competing Commitments** I may also be committed to . . . being seen as successful, not being overwhelmed, not being found out to be a fraud, a phony, and not being rejected	I assume that if people discovered I was a fraud then . . . • I would be shamed, • I would not be valued, • I would have no meaningful conversations, • I would be isolated, alone, rejected, lonely and forgotten, • I would have no legacy, I would make no difference, and • I would not fulfill my life purpose.

EXAMPLE 6. ON NOT BEING IN CONTROL

COLUMN 0	COLUMN 1	COLUMN 2	COLUMN 3	COLUMN 4
COMPLAINTS OR FRUSTRATIONS (What shouldn't be)	NOBLE COMMITMENT (Improvement Goal)	DOING OR NOT DOING INSTEAD	COMPETING COMMITMENTS	BIG ASSUMPTIONS CORE BELIEFS
Elders shouldn't be duped and believing their life doesn't matter. They should be respected. They should matter to themselves and to others.	I am committed to being a real person and doing my own soul will work. I am committed to value myself and being of value.	Instead of doing my own personal work, I . . . spend my time taking care of others, manage a board, help others develop their careers, go to too many meetings, and take over jobs that others should be doing.	**Worry Box** I won't look like I'm doing my job. People won't like me. The real me won't be good enough. **Competing Commitments** I may also be committed to . . . being in control, being admired, and being the center of attention.	I assume if I was not in control . . . • everything would fall apart, • I would know what to do with myself, and • I would not appear to be competent and would be relegated to mowing lawns, • I would not feel valued, • I would isolate myself and drink too much, and • my life would crumble and I would be an immense pain and sorrow.

extended transcript of a psychodrama

TRANSCRIPT

REVIEW OF NOBLE AND COMPETING COMMITMENTS

BEGIN PSYCHODRAMA

ROUND 1: CATHARSIS

ROUND 2: JUSTIFYING OUR THE COMPETING COMMITMENTS

ROUND 3: FORGIVENESS

Transcript

Psychodrama has proved to be one of the more powerful tools of Transformational Inquiry. My presentation in chapter 5 was far too brief to give the sense of its power. Below is a transcript of an extended psychodrama. I have kept most of the original dialog so you can get the flavor of how we move in and out of roles. It is typical to step out of character to reflect on the process or to help the Participant go more deeply into his or her role. You will notice in Round 3 that I stop frequently to help Patty (not her real name) express compassion and forgiveness toward her self-protective Competing Commitment. This is common in psychodramas. We are so unaccustomed to seeing our Competing Commitments in this light that it can take a lot of redirecting. You will also notice that the focus drifts. This is also common as new insights emerge in the course of psychodrama and are incorporated into the role-playing.

We begin by reviewing Patty's Immunity to Change. We have done a good deal of work together, so I am a directing her more to get us started on the psychodrama. Also, this psychodrama was conducted individually, so we are lacking the input from a group.

Review of Noble and Competing Commitments

Tom: *What is your first column commitment?*

Patty: *My commitment is to be a good parent. And then my other commitment is to have a life outside of parenting.*

Tom: *So to be a good parent and to have a life outside of parenting?*

Patty: *Yes, to be a good parent and have a life outside . . . that is if your kids don't have any special issues, that's how I see it.*

Tom: *So let's think through it in terms of the four columns. You said, "I'd like to be a good parent and have a life outside of that." That's your Column 1 Commitment. So what are you doing or not doing to keep that from happening?*

Patty: *I'm stressing when the kids are having issues. Whenever their medication is not working as I think it should be working, or whatever the teacher emails me about one of the kids . . . I hate that I can't bend but get blown about with the wind, like that.*

Tom: *So what if you didn't allow yourself to be blown about by the wind? In other words, what if you didn't respond with anxiety and worry if something happened?*

Patty: *I think that, I really think that I would be letting my kids down by not working as hard as I could to make their life better. So if I just take it easy and say that's just the way the chips fall, I would be irresponsible. Not only do I not want to be irresponsible, I don't want to fail! I'm spending my whole time, my life, parenting, my 30s, my 40s, whatever, parenting. Who wants to spend their time and find out that they failed?*

Tom: *Yes, I understand that fear. So what would happen if you did fail?*

Patty: *So then I would lead a life of . . . I mean then what would be the meaning of my life? That sort of implies that you don't have meaning in your life until the results come in. That doesn't seem right does it (laughing)?*

Tom: *No, (laughing) but that's perfect in terms of a Big Assumption, because the nature of the Big Assumption is what you're talking about now:* "If I failed, my life wouldn't have any meaning. It would be just kind of empty and purposeless." *Which is probably a very accurate statement of your Big Assumption. And when you look at it with the rational mind you say,* "that's just stupid!" *(Laughing together) but it's just the most natural thing in the world . . .that story still runs very deeply.*

Patty: *Yeah, I'm living in this life and I have a narrative going in my head, and I'm in the middle of the book, and there's a conclusion that I'm going to be in charge, depending on how I do it. It'll turn out okay or it'll turn out badly. But that's not really how I should view life. I should view it as a narrative story with arc . . .that's not how life works.*
. . .So I think I'm reading life in the wrong way.

Tom: *Maybe you are reading life in the wrong way. What we try to get to in this work is that you got a story very very early on that said,* "if I fail, it's a disaster!" *Somewhere you got that story and it went very deep. In my experience, the nature of those stories is that they are typically wrong, and not very functional. But they were formed when we were innocent, young children who couldn't know better. We didn't choose these stories with our wonderful rational minds.*

Patty: *It could've been that I could have chosen to view my adoption, my abandonment, as a failure on my part. And I probably did to some extent because I suppose other people are not quite so worried about failing.*

Tom: *A lot of others are.*

Patty: *They don't seem as bothered . . .*

Begin Psychodrama
Round 1: Catharsis

Tom: *Shall we do a psychodrama and walk into it?*

Patty: *Yeah*

Tom: *Here are the roles we will play for this. I will play the role of your Competing Commitment/Big Assumption around the whole issue of being a failure. In this first round you get to just get pissed at me.*

Patty: *So you're going to be the person who thinks that failure is the worst thing in the world?*

Tom: *Yes, so I'm sort of the third and fourth column, I'm in that role. And you will be the Noble Commitment, the one who wants to live and have this larger life and not be so anxious. You would like to get free of this anxiety. Does that work all right for you? Is that an accurate statement of the issue for you?*

Patty: *Yeah, I'd like to not focus on the things that the kids do wrong. Or the things that happen that are bad. I'd like to be able to have a broader perspective, a broader outlook on what life entails.*

Tom: *So the opportunity in this first round is for you to get really mad at me. I'm going to play the role of keeping you from what you want. It's your opportunity to yell at me, scream at me, and say whatever you would like to me. Because I'm the one keeping you from having the life you want!*

Patty (stepping into the role of the **Noble Commitment**): *So why are you doing that then? Why are you hindering me from . . . Why are you always there telling me how to behave?*

Competing Commitment (Tom): *Well, you see if I didn't do that your life would be a disaster! You'll just ruin it.*

Patty: *But other people don't have someone on their shoulder like you . . .Always being negative, always looking at the bad! You feel like you have to be one step ahead or something really bad is going to happen. But other people don't feel that way! You don't need to be there.*

Competing Commitment (Tom): *You're right and it'll be okay. But if you fail, it will be a complete disaster! Our lives would just crumble! You're not like other people you know. You're really not, other people can fail*

Patty: *Well, first of all would that necessarily be failing?*

Tom: (stepping out of the role of the Competing Commitment): *Don't be rational with me, I invite you to just get pissed off at me. I'll be as obnoxious as I can.*

Patty: *So what's wrong with failing? People fail all the time! Even famous people fail!*

Tom: (back in the role of the Competing Commitment): *Yeah but if you fail, you'll just think about* I'm not any better than anyone else . . .

Competing Commitment (Tom): *But just think about it if you fail, IF YOU FAIL! You will have spent all of this time raising these kids and your life will mean nothing. NOTHING! God, what a disaster that would be!*

Patty: *But I see people who are great people and they have a wonderful life, and they have kids that they don't have control over. And their kids might be doing drugs, might be going to jail—am I to say that they failed? I don't think that they failed. I don't think they failed their kids. I think the only way you can fail your kids is by not loving them.*

Competing Commitment (Tom): *Yeah but they have resources we don't have.*

Patty: *I have a lot of resources!*

Competing Commitment (Tom): *Oh . . . I don't know. Just imagine, you're fortysomething and the kids are grown, you haven't done anything except raise kids. Neither one can take care of themselves, they're in trouble, why would you have put all of your life and . . .?*

Patty: *God has a purpose for everybody and just because they're not perfect doesn't mean they can't be good people.*

Tom: *Okay let's take a timeout for a moment. I'm trying to rile you up and you're responding with rational answers. If we had our support group here they would be behind you yelling at me. I'm inviting you to actually get angry at me.*

Patty: *The hard part is that I hear you (in your role as my Competing Commitment), and I agree with you. So I'm trying to not agree with you . . . This is the hard part for me, to push back against you.*

Tom: *You're pushing back rationally.*

Patty: *Yes, it seems the only way I can see it. My internal instinct is "Yeah he's right."*

Tom: *Is there a part of you that really got angry at me for saying these things?*

Patty: *Yeah, I think so. I'm not angry mad . . . It just shouldn't be that way. I shouldn't have to be mad. I shouldn't have to have you on my shoulder like that. And have that be the only way that I can live. I should be able to live a good life without having all this excessive worry.*

Tom (Back in the role of the **Competing Commitment**): *All right let's step in.. Tell me about that. I'm trying to protect you!*

Patty: *You're trying to protect me?! You're not protecting me, you're raising my stress levels by acting like this, by always being on my back like this! I can't handle it really! Because I get very depressed. And this just makes me more depressed. You need to back off! You need to let me be who I can be without you there.*

(She's starting to feel some real anger here, which is good.)

Competing Commitment (Tom): Oh, that would be a disaster.

Patty: *I think I could handle it without you! You think you're so important, and I really just don't see how you're helping me!*

Competing Commitment (Tom): *I may not be helping you, but I am protecting you from a disaster, an utter disaster! If you don't stay on top of this,* *if you don't make sure this is right . . .*

Patty: (interrupting) *I can do this without you! I don't need somebody standing over me telling me when to worry and when not to worry. I can—I can take what's going on and look at it. And make my decisions from the actions that have happened. But you step in, and you bring a whole emotional aspect to it. And I can't get beyond the emotions. So you just need to step aside and let me look at things as they come!*

Competing Commitment (Tom): *Nah, I don't think so.*

Patty: *Emotions hinder (laughing) . . . In this case. It's stopping me from living my life the way I want to live it!*

Tom: (stepping out of role as Competing Commitment): *Good, very good! That was great!*

Patty: *Well . . .*

Tom: *You want to keep going? Okay, let's keep going.* (Stepping back into the role of Competing Commitment). *Now you know you can't do it, really.*

Patty: *You said I can't do it but there's no reason why I can't do this, no reason why I can't just take things that happen and look at them from that perspective and bring in that whole emotional worry to it. You want to bring the worry in. I don't know how you expect that to help. I don't know where that's coming from.*

Competing Commitment (Tom): *So, if you failed it would be just like when we were adopted. That was so horrible! It'd be just like that all over again!*

Patty: *But you're looking at that the wrong way! I didn't feel bad when I was adopted! I was actually adopted into a really great family. It wasn't a failure, I don't know why my mom couldn't keep me but I know it wasn't a failure on my part!*

Competing Commitment (Tom): *If that happened again . . . We would just be ruined! We would be destroyed!*

Patty: *No! My relationship with my kids is completely different than my mom's relationship with me, my birth mom. To connect this is ridiculous. . . To say that my adoption has anything to do with what I'm going through now.*

Competing Commitment (Tom): *You just don't understand, you just don't understand! We can't do this again! We can't go down this path again!*

Patty: *I'm not going down the path again. I'm going down a whole new path. And I can go down this path very well without you trying to bend it back towards my adoption!*

Competing Commitment (Tom): *I'm not bending it back toward your adoption. I'm trying to protect you! I'm trying to keep you from . . . well . . . If we failed again, our life would just crumble, it would just fall apart.*

Patty: *Whatever happens with my kids, I know I'm doing the best I can! I have to do the best I can anyway, whether you're there or not. And if you being there makes it harder, I still gotta do the best I can. In doing the best I can, I know I haven't failed. Whatever happens to my kids, I still haven't failed!*

Tom (stepping out of role as Competing Commitment): Bravo! That was excellent! Okay let's trade places.

ROUND 2: JUSTIFYING OUR COMPETING COMMITMENTS

At this point, Tom and Patty move to opposite sides of the table. Tom is now in the role of the Noble Commitment and Patty is in the position of the Competing Commitment.

Tom: *That was good! I don't think I've seen you express it that clearly before.*

Patty: *Yeah, I'm thinking about . . .You know I think that, but to say it out loud like that. That makes it more real. It's so true, I can only affect so much. But if I'm doing the best I can, that's all I can expect of me, that's all God can expect of me. And that's not failing . . .*

Tom: *What I'm going to ask you to do now is shift roles. Now you're going to be in the role of the Competing Commitment.*

Patty: *That's easier for me. I'm more used to this role.*

Tom: *Okay, you ready to dive in? I will play the Noble Commitment, and you will be the Competing Commitment.*

Patty: (as the Competing Commitment): *You know, if you don't worry about what's going to happen to the kids you haven't done the best you can. And if you haven't done the best you can then you have failed.*

Noble Commitment (Tom): *Get back! That's not true! How could I have failed?*

Patty: *Because you're not doing the best you can. The only way you can do the best you can is by thinking about it all the time! By thinking and trying to figure out the best solution. You're in charge, you're their mom.*

Noble Commitment (Tom): *Yeah but worrying about it all the time is not any a help. You just want me to worry.*

Patty: *If you're not going to worry, you're not going to think about it. And if you don't think about it, you're not going to be able to help.*

Noble Commitment (Tom): *So then if I'm not worried about the kids all the time then I'm going to abandon them?*

Patty: *Yeah that's basically abandoning them if you don't worry about them! How else are you going to take care of them?*

Noble Commitment (Tom):*Now wait a minute, that doesn't work out. I want my life. I want to have a whole, healthy life and not just be always caught up and worried about them. That doesn't serve them, or me!*

Patty: *You've had kids for eleven years, and you've done nothing but worry about them. And you are surviving just fine that way.*

Noble Commitment (Tom): *Wow! No, I'm not actually. I want to do better than this. I don't want to be stressed all the time. And you keep me being stressed! And I can't see that it's helping anything.*

Patty: *I'm keeping the kids . . . I'm helping by keeping the kids from going down the wrong path. I can list a couple of decisions that, because of my worry, helped improve their lives.*

Noble Commitment (Tom): *Okay, so tell me.*

Patty: *So, because of my worry about Jimmy we got an autism diagnosis.*

Noble Commitment (Tom): *We couldn't have got that without anxiety and worry?*

Patty: *I pushed you . . . I pushed you to get that diagnosis. It's the anxiety and the worry that keeps me thinking about it all night long, keeps me thinking about it during the day. I try to figure out solutions. I don't know that you would come up with a solution if you didn't have me worrying.*

Noble Commitment (Tom): *You could have given me 30 seconds with the worry and I would've written down "Okay get Jimmy tested," then we could be done with it. I don't need you all the time. You're so scared . . .*

Patty: *No! I'm not scared. I just know that we don't want to fail again; we don't want to fail our kids!*

Noble Commitment (Tom): *So what would happen if we failed?*

Patty: *If we failed, our lives would be meaningless! Who wants to live a failed life? Who wants to live a life where what you did was meaningless? That's nobody's dream. You want to have kids? It's your responsibility to make sure that they get the best that they can.*

Noble Commitment (Tom): *Oh yeah, but would I just be worried about it all the time? What help is that?*

Patty: *Worrying about it makes you look into solutions.*

Noble Commitment (Tom): *I can look into solutions without being worried.*

(Notice that we are going in circles here. We are enacting a conversation that goes on in Patty's head off and on throughout the day. As we go around and around we help make that which was *subject* to her into an *object* for her consideration.)

Patty: *I don't think you would take it seriously if you weren't worried about it, though.*

Noble Commitment (Tom): *Oh, so I have to be worried and have a meaningless life so we can keep from failing to take care of my kids?*

Patty: *Yeah*

Noble Commitment (Tom): *I'm not buyin' that . . . I'm not buyin' that! That's silly! That's just nuts! I don't want your help . . . I don't need your help!*

Patty: *If you didn't have worry on your side then you wouldn't think of it in a serious enough manner and your kids would suffer the consequences. And it wouldn't be you, it would be your kids! You want that on your shoulders?*

Noble Commitment (Tom): *So, the kids don't do as well as I think they might, they take a different path. So what?*

Patty: *Well, it's about you! So what's the point of being a parent if you can't keep your kids from harm or you can't make their life better?*

Tom (stepping out of the role of Competing Commitment):*Let's pause for a second. I'm trying to invite you into . . . What is it you're protecting me (the Noble Commitment) from? What would happen to us if I really didn't pay attention to your anxiety?*

Patty: *If I didn't pay attention to my anxiety, then I would not seriously . . . I wouldn't consider myself as seriously thinking about solutions for helping the kids in solving the problems they have. And if I didn't seriously think about solutions then I am not being a good parent. I'm not doing the best I can. And the only way I can do the best I can is by worrying. Which isn't necessarily true.*

Tom: *And if we did fail, it would just be a meaningless life?*

Patty: *Yeah it would be like . . . What's the point of us having kids if they don't turn out . . .In my story arc I've got an idea of what my kids are going to be like, I think. And it's so unknown to me, it scares me. Because I don't know what Jimmy's future is going to be like. I know Susie is probably going to be fine. But Jimmy, I don't know what his future is going to be like. And I feel like I'm an instrument of his success or failure. And I need to step it up. And the only way I can step it up is by constantly thinking about it. And by constantly thinking about it, I worry about it.*

Tom: *You said that very clearly, that was beautiful!*

Patty: *Yeah, that's where the worry comes from. I'm not being responsible if I don't worry! Worrying means I'm responsible! . . . I never said it like that before.*

Tom: *Yes that's very clear! That was beautiful. What I hear is that, on the one hand, if I don't spend all my time worrying about the kids I'm wasting my time and not living up to my expectations. And if I do spend all my time worrying about my kids and not taking care of my own life I'm wasting my time.*

Patty: *Yeah, yeah, they're like balancing each other out. Yeah, worry to me is like responsibility. And yet I'm also responsible for my well-being has a human, not just as a parent.*

Tom: *You're getting some good insights*

Patty: *Yeah I thought I probably would. And I'm still worried about my kids. It is not Susie, its Jimmy. I can't think about other things until the issues with Jimmy are resolved, but I'm confused because I don't know what to do . . . I'm still consumed by those sorts of things. I still wonder if having a job outside of the home would be good, because then I'd have other things to focus on. But then, I wonder, if I'd be even more stressed because I have more on my plate.*

Round 3: Forgiveness

Tom: *So let's change positions, and I will play in the **worry** role. What I want you to do this time is to reach out to me in that role with compassion. I want you to see me a little differently.*

Patty: *Not being antagonistic towards you . . .*

Tom: *Yes, I'm going to invite you to see me as kind of a younger version of you, a little child that's frightened . . . who is protecting us from a disaster. So reach out to me and invite me to tell the story of you and see if you can see me a little bit differently, with forgiveness and compassion.*

Patty: *Okay*

Competing Commitment (Tom): *I'm so scared! If you go off on your own and do these things, like get a job . . . I'm so scared that if you do that our life will crumble. That the kids will grow up and not be able to take care of themselves.*

Patty: *Yeah, I hear you. I want to go off, and I really think I should go off and do other things. But I know where you're coming from.*

Competing Commitment (Tom): *I don't think you do because if you did* *you wouldn't even be thinking about this.*

Patty: *I think I have a responsibility towards you to understand why you're worried. And I can see that you have a lot of anxiety.*

Competing Commitment (Tom): *Yeah ,you're just being nice to me now.* (Laughter)

Patty: *Yeah, that's true.* (more laughter)

Competing Commitment (Tom): *Just think about it, Susie's out there, a troublemaker and she's just so flamboyant that people don't want her around. Oh they'll look at me and they'll say,* "She's such a bad mom, she doesn't know how to raise her daughter right."

Patty: *I think you're taking on so much responsibility, probably more responsibility then you need to.*

Competing Commitment (Tom): *Well if I don't, you won't! Then what'll happen?*

Patty: *Then Susie will live her life. She's going to be who she is. You're responsible for giving her what she needs, but you're not responsible for changing her behavior. But you want to be changing her behavior.*

Competing Commitment (Tom): *I am, I'm responsible for all of that! If she doesn't turn out right, it's my fault! You don't get it! You don't get it! If she doesn't turn out right, that's our fault. People will look at us, they won't like us. They'll criticize us.*

Patty: *Whose opinion really matters?*

Tom (stepping out of the role of Competing Commitment): Okay, let's pause here. You're defending your position. What I invite you to do is to reach out to me in my fear. Try holding my hand while we talk.

Patty: *Okay*

Patty (moving back into the role of the Noble Commitment): *I understand you feel like you have a lot of responsibility on your shoulders. A huge amount of responsibility, and you don't realize you don't need to be responsible for everything that happens.*

Competing Commitment (Tom): *If I didn't worry, you wouldn't do things right!*

Patty: *I don't know that you have to worry as hard as you do. Can you worry a little bit less?*

Competing Commitment (Tom): *If I were in this less it'll just go down the tubes.*

Tom (in an aside reflecting on his role): *Let me tell you what I would like to hear* (in the role of the self-protective Competing Commitments): "*I understand that you're scared, sweetheart. I understand that you're terrified. But I'll be here, I'll take care of you.*"

Patty: *Oh, you want me to take care of you. You want me to be there for you. You know I can take care of you though. If you're so worried . . .I don't want you to be worried. I want you there with me because I think . . .Because you give me responsibility. But I don't need you to worry as hard as you do. I still want you around. I don't want you go away completely.*

Competing Commitment (Tom with hesitation): *Uh, okay. I didn't know that. I thought you just want to get rid of me. Get me out of your life so you can go party or whatever you're going to do.*

Patty: *No, I think we need to have a real good partnership. You really care about the kids. I see that, you care about the kids more than you care about yourself. And you see me as caring more about myself than the kids. We need to meet, we need to come together at a point where we're both happy together. I really need you by me. And . . . I need you as a voice in my head, not as an emotion in my heart. I need you there, I don't want to abandon you. I don't want you to go away completely. Because I think you really have good things to offer.*

Competing Commitment (Tom): *I'm so scared . . .I'm so scared . . . Not only would our life just be miserable, but we'd be a big failure. I do so much to protect us and you just ignore me . . . You just ignore me. (Big sigh).*

Patty: *You're trying to protect us . . .That's awesome. I see you doing that. And that's a huge undertaking. No wonder you're worried all the time when you feel all the burden is on you.*

Competing Commitment (Tom): *What I want is for you to just care* *about me to . . . want you to take care of me to . . . Just let me know . . . That it's okay . . . Somehow . . .that you're not going to abandon me. That I won't get lost.*

Tom (stepping out of role): *Let's pause here. What I'm inviting you to do is reach out emotionally to me. Kind of embrace me. Let me know that I'm okay . . .I want to be emotionally embraced by you and protected. I'm carrying this horrible burden.*

Patty (picking up the role): *You're kind of like the little girl I was. You had to go through a lot. But you don't have to be a little girl that has to please everybody all the time. You're not going to disappear if that happens.*

Competing Commitment (Tom): *Oh, I don't know if I believe you.*

Patty: *You, you've changed . . . You're not that little girl anymore.*

Tom (again stepping out of role): *What I want to hear from you in this role is* "I will take care of you, I will be here for you no matter what. I will take care of you . . . "

Patty (picking up the role): *You're like my kids, I can take care of you. You don't have to take care of me. You don't have to try and do all that. I'll be there for you.*

Competing Commitment (Tom): *Will you listen to me?*

Patty: *I will listen to you. And when you talk to me I will hear you. And I don't need you to have answers for everything. You can just talk.*

Competing Commitment (Tom): *I want you to hear me. I don't want you to be as scared as I am.*

Patty: *No, I don't need to be as scared as you are. . . . I'll take care of you. You don't need to worry about me not being able to take of you.*

Competing Commitment (Tom): *Yeah, I needed you to not be as scared as me. I don't like living being the scared all the time. And when you get scared about me being scared, then I get more scared.*

Patty: *But I can take care of the kids and I can take care of you. And we can be together, you don't have to go away. Okay?*

Tom (stepping out of role): *How you doing right now?*

Patty: *I'm trying to be that maternal comforter, which is hard for me because I'm the one that usually needs the comfort. And I'm really trying to believe that I'm the person that can give the comfort to somebody. (Long pause).*

Tom: *What do you feel about this persona (Competing Commitment) feeling so scared?*

Patty: *I think that's a new way for me to look at that persona. I don't see that persona as being scared, I see it as being hard-core.*

Tom: *Why?*

Patty: *Maybe she is scared. . . . What was she scared of earlier, not doing the right thing? Maybe if she'd done the right thing she wouldn't have been abandoned. Maybe if she'd been the right kind of person, her mother would have kept her. If I can do the right thing by my kids, then they will turn out. It's a scary thing to look at. I mean, it's like so much is stacked . . . It's so important.*

Tom (stepping back into the role of the Competing Commitment): *I wonder if one of the things I'm afraid of is my children being abandoned the way I was.*

Patty: *Not abandoned by me!*

Tom (out of role): *Not abandoned, but kind of rejected.*

Patty: *Oh, yeah . . . That's a really good point! A lot of my protection has to do with Susie having a lot of friends and not feeling loneliness, like she's not good enough . . . I want her to feel like she's normal.*

Tom (outside of role): *So, where are you right now?*

Patty: *I'm just kind of wrapping my head around it all right now. I'm thinking of all the things I haven't thought of before. Like worrying about them being abandoned. The whole idea that I can't be responsible unless I worry.*

For another ten or fifteen minutes Patty and I discussed our conversations and the new insights she had gained.

appendix e:

byron katie worksheets

WORKSHEET 1: JUDGE-YOUR-NEIGHBOR WORKSHEET

WORKSHEET 2: ONE-BELIEF-AT-A-TIME WORKSHEET

WORKSHEET 1

THE WORK OF BYRON KATIE   ## Judge-Your-Neighbor Worksheet

Judge your neighbor • Write it down • Ask four questions • Turn it around

Fill in the blanks below, writing about someone (dead or alive) you haven't yet forgiven one hundred percent. Use short, simple sentences. Don't censor yourself—try to fully experience the anger or pain as if the situation were occurring right now. Take this opportunity to express your judgments on paper.

1. In this situation, time, and location, who angers, confuses, or disappoints you, and why?

I am _____ with _____ because _____
       emotion   *name*

Example: I am angry with Paul because he doesn't listen to me about his health.

2. In this situation, how do you want them to change? What do you want them to do?

I want _____ to _____
        name

Example: I want Paul to see that he is wrong. I want him to stop lying to me. I want him to see that he is killing himself.

3. In this situation, what advice would you offer to them?

_____ should/shouldn't _____
    name

Example: Paul should take a deep breath. He should calm down. He should see that his behavior frightens me. He should know that being right is not worth another heart attack.

4. In order for *you* to be happy in this situation, what do you need them to think, say, feel, or do?

I need _____ to _____
      name

Example: I need Paul to hear me when I talk to him. I need him to take care of himself. I need him to admit that I am right.

5. What do you think of them in this situation? Make a list.

_____ is _____
    name

Example: Paul is unfair, arrogant, loud, dishonest, way out of line, and unconscious.

6. What is it in or about this situation that you don't ever want to experience again?

I don't ever want _____

Example: I don't ever want Paul to lie to me again. I don't ever want to see him ruining his health again.

Now investigate each of the above statements using the four questions. Always give yourself time to let the deeper answers meet the questions. Then turn each thought around. For the turnaround to statement 6, replace the words "I don't ever want to ..." with "I am willing to ..." and "I look forward to ..." Until you can look forward to all aspects of life without fear, your Work is not done.

The four questions
Example: Paul doesn't listen to me about his health.
1. **Is it true?** (Yes or no. If no, move to 3.)
2. **Can you absolutely know that it's true?** (Yes or no.)
3. **How do you react, what happens, when you believe that thought?**
4. **Who would you be without the thought?**

Turn the thought around
a) **to the self.** (*I don't listen to myself about my health.*)
b) **to the other.** (*I don't listen to Paul about his health.*)
c) **to the opposite.** (*Paul does listen to me about his health.*)
Then find at least three specific, genuine examples of how each turnaround is true for you in this situation.

For more information on how to do The Work, visit thework.com

Rev. 25 Jul. 2014

WORKSHEET 2

THE WORK
of Byron Katie®

One-Belief-at-a-Time Worksheet
The Work—A Written Meditation

On the line below, write down a stressful concept about someone (alive or dead) whom you haven't forgiven 100 percent. (For example, "He doesn't care about me" or "I did it wrong.") Then question the concept in writing, using the following questions and turnarounds. (Use additional paper as needed.) When answering the questions, close your eyes, be still, and witness what appears to you. Inquiry stops working the moment you stop answering the questions.

Belief: _____

1. **Is it true?** (Yes or no. If no, move to question 3.)

   _____

2. **Can you absolutely know that it's true?** (Yes or no.)

   _____

3. **How do you react, what happens, when you believe that thought?**

   _____
   _____

   a) Does that thought bring peace or stress into your life?

   _____
   _____

   b) What images do you see, past and future, and what physical sensations arise as you think that thought and witness those images?

   _____
   _____
   _____

   c) What emotions arise when you believe that thought? (Refer to the Emotions List, available on thework.com.)

   _____
   _____
   _____

   d) Do any obsessions or addictions begin to appear when you believe that thought? (Do you act out on any of the following: alcohol, drugs, credit cards, food, sex, television?)

   _____
   _____
   _____

   e) How do you treat the person in this situation when you believe the thought? How do you treat other people and yourself?

   _____
   _____
   _____
   _____
   _____
   _____
   _____
   _____
   _____
   _____
   _____
   _____

Endnotes

1   Al Gore, *The Future: Six Drivers of Global Change.* (New York: Random House 2013), xv.

2   Ibid., xiv.

3   Rebecca D. Costa, *The Watchman's Rattle: Thinking Our Way Out of Extinction.* (Philadelphia, PA: Vanguard Press), 9.

4   Robert Kegan, *In Over Our Heads: The Mental Demands of Modern Life.* (Cambridge, Mass: Harvard University Press, 1994), 185-197.

5   Costa, 9.

6   Ibid., 12.

7   Ibid., p 13.

8   Ibid., p 30.

9   This metaphor was so important to Fuller that he had it engraved on his tombstone: "call me trim tab."

10   Integral Ministry is dedicated to evolving human consciousness and uses Integral theory has its map. Tom was ordained by OUnI, The Order of Interfaith Interspiritual Integral Ministry in 2012.

11   See Ken Wilber, *Integral Spirituality, (City, Publisher, Date).*

12   *Widgets* is the economist's generalized term for any product of service offered by a business of other entity

13   http://en.wikipedia.org/wiki/Consciousness

14   See Appendix A for a more in-depth exploration of the theoretical foundation of Transformational Inquiry and of how it is contextualized within Integral _____.

15   Chögyam Trungpa, *Crazy Wisdom,* J. L. Lief, S. Chödzin (eds.)

(Boston: Shambhala Publications, 2001). ISBN 0-87773-910-2. Citation taken from Wikipedia.

16   For extensive development of Immunity to Change see: *How The Way We Talk Can Change the Way We Work* and *Immunity to Change.*

17   Peter L. Berger, "Western Individuality: Liberation and Loneliness," *Partisan Review* 52 (1985). From http://www3.dbu.edu/mITChell/modernit.htm

18   Robert Kegan and Lisa Laskow Lahey, *Immunity to Change: How to Overcome It and Unlock the Potential in Yourself and Your Organization.* (Boston, Massachusetts: Harvard Business Press, 2009).

19   Robert Kegan and Lisa Laskow Lahey, *How the Way We talk Can Change the Way We Work.* (San Francisco: Jossey-Bass, 2001

20   Ibid., 1

21   Robert Kegan and Lisa Laskow Lahey, *Immunity to Change: How to Overcome It and Unlock the Potential in Yourself and Your Organization.* (Boston, Massachusetts: Harvard Business Press, 2009).

22   This section is derived from the workbook created by Kegan and Lahey for their facilitator trainings: "ITC Facilitator's Workshop: Guide to the *Immunity to Change* Exercise, 2011 Edition."

23   See Appendix A for a more thorough discussion of technical and adaptive change.

24   Op. cit., 134.

25   Kegan and Lahey, (2009), p. 261

26   See Robert Kegan and Lisa Laskow Lahey, **How the Way We talk Can Change the Way We Work.** (San Francisco: Jossey-Bass, 2001) and Robert Kegan and Lisa Laskow Lahey, **Immunity to Change: How to Overcome It and Unlock the Potential in Yourself and Your Organization,** (Boston, Massachusetts: Harvard Business Press, 2009). If you want to dive into the theory, see Kegan's **In Over our Heads: The Mental Demands of Modern Life.** (Cambridge, MA: Harvard University Press, 1998).

27   Tom Thresher: **Reverent Irreverence: Integral Church for the 21st Century, from Cradle to Christ Consciousness** (City: Integral Press, 2009)

28   See Appendix A for an integral orientation on development.

29   David Loy. **Lack and Transcendence** (Amherst, NY: Prometheus Books/Humanity Books, 2000)

30   Aldous Huxley, *The Perennial Philosophy* (New York: Harper Perennial Modern Classics 2004), p. 1

31 Lynn Bauman, *The Gospel of Thomas: Wisdom of the* Twin (Ashland, OR: White Cloud Press, 2012), p. 9.

32 Gospel of Luke, 11:2

33 Tom Cheetham, *All the World an Icon: Henry Corbin and the Angelic Function of Beings*. (Berkeley, California: North Atlantic books, 2012), 68.

34 This summary is adapted from a wonderful article written by K. Lauren de Boer entitled "New Cosmology: A Great Story—Our Common Story" by *YES! Magazine*, issue number, page number posted February 21, 2006. http://www.yesmagazine.org/issues/10-most-hopeful-trends/new-cosmology-a-great-story-our-common-story.

35 Ibid.

36 Ibid.

37 http://www.amitgoswami.org/

38 Ibid.

39 The Quantum Activist Workbook http://www.quantumactivist.com/media/QA-WorkBook3.pdf. 3

40 Ibid., 5.

41 Ibid., 18.

42 Ibid., 19.

43 Ibid., 21.

44 A quick from Einstein regarding quantum mechanics notion of nonlocality.

45 December 2013

46 Cynthia Bourgeault, *The Holy Trinity and the Law of Three: Discovering the Radical Truth at the Heart of Christianity* (Boston: Shambhala, 2013), 15.

47 ibid., 16.

48 ibid.

49 ibid., 26.

50 ibid., 40.

51 The following is an abridged version from my previous book: *Reverent Irreverence: Integral Church for the 21st Century, from Cradle to Christ-Consciousness,(City: Publisher, Date)*

52 Lynn Baumann. *Gospel of Thomas*. Emphasis added

53 Erik Vance, "Why Nothing Works," *Discover Magazine*, July/August 2014, 43.

54 http://www.adyashanti.org/index.php?file=writings_inner&writingid=41

55 Ephesians 5:13 – 14.

56 Jonathan Haidt. *The Righteous Mind: Why Good People Are Divided by Politics and Religion.* (New York, Penguin books, 2012).

57 Ibid, p63.

58 Byron Katie. *Loving What Is: Four Questions That Can Change Your Life.* Three Rivers Press; December 23, 2003.

59 As indicated in Chapter 8 Participants pre-class work is to consider a change that would make an important difference to their lives. We can use this information to help clarify their Column 1 Noble Commitment.

60 Byron Katie. *Loving What Is: Four Questions That Can Change Your Life.* Three Rivers Press; December 23, 2003.

61 See www.CommonHouse.us or like CommonHouse on Facebook

62 [2] For elaboration of this orientation see *Reverent Irreverence: Integral Church for the 21st Century, from Cradle to Christ-Consciousness*

63 The titles used here come from my previous book *Reverent Irreverence: Integral Church for the 21st Century, from Cradle to Christ-Consciousness.*

64 [4] The Unitive/Transpersonal wave of development is actually the beginning of a third tier path of development. The third tier points to evolution of the individual beyond their identification with ego.

65 See *Reverent Irreverence: Integral Church for the 21st Century, from Cradle to Christ-Consciousness* (Integral Publishers, 2010) and *Integral Spirituality: A Startling New Role for Religion in the Modern and Postmodern World* (Shambhala, 2007).

66 Robert Kegan, Lisa Laskow Lahey. *Immunity to Change: How to Overcome It and Unlock the Potential in Yourself and Your Organization.* (Boston, Harvard Business Press, 2009), p11

67 ibid. 19

68 ibid., emphasis in the original

69 ibid. 20

70 ibid. 29

71 ibid.

72 ibid.

73 ibid. 47

74 to the

75 ibid.

76 ibid.

77 ibid. 48

78 ibid. emphasis added

79 ibid. 50 emphasis added

80 A question, of course, the tools in this book are meant to answer.

81 ibid. 51 emphasis in the original

82 Ibid 54

about the author

Tom has spent more than a dozen years leading groups and individuals through Transformational Inquiry. He has watched with delight as individuals made important personal changes in the nascent integral church he pastors, as well as in the Leadership and Personal Development Program for the Bainbridge Graduate Institute (which offers an MBA degree in sustainable business).

His work is grounded in eight years of intensive transformational practice during his twenties. Tom has an eclectic background. He holds a PhD in Education and an MA in Economics from Stanford University. After teaching economics for more than a decade, he spent twelve years as an artist/craftsman, creating inlaid clocks from exotic hardwoods, and later crafting kaleidoscopes in alabaster.

A surprising call to ministry led to a M.Div. and fifteen years leading faith communities. His twenty-year study of integral theory, his efforts to create an integral church, and his book, *Reverent Irreverence: Integral Church for the 21st Century, from Cradle to Christ-Consciousness* led to his ordination as the country's second Integral Minister.

Tom is a compelling, dynamic teacher. His irreverent sense of humor creates an easy-going atmosphere for the participants in his classes. He is available for trainings, facilitations and speaking engagements. For more information, see **www.transformationalinquiry.us** or contact him at tomthresher@comcast.net.

PRAISE FOR CRAZY WISDOM

"A superb, fully integrally-informed guide through the tried and tested techniques developed by Robert Kegan and his associates for undermining and releasing resistance to change. Most change technologies don't work very well because they never deal with the prior, hidden, unconscious patterns that are committed to NOT changing—yet only by dealing with those can real change occur—in any area. This is what Tom Thresher's new book does. It is especially developed for people in faith communities, so if you are Spirit-oriented, not to worry!—(but it works in any event). If you're serious about introducing real change in your life, this is the place to start!"

—Ken Wilber—The Fourth Turning and The Integral Vision

"We are proud to call Tom Thresher a colleague, and we heartily recommend this book to any person or community looking to nourish the soul."

—Robert Kegan and Lisa Lahey, authors of Immunity to Change

"At a time when change is a constant and there is a deep hunger for meaning, connection, and relationship within communities of faith, Tom Thresher's work reminds us to move into our resistance with courage, compassion and a sense of our own identity. The relevance of "Crazy Wisdom" cannot be overstated. Foundationally we each find our elephants in charge and a reframing of our thoughts, worries, assumptions and fears assists us in moving forward into change, into the new, and into the goals and commitments we wish to make for ourselves and our communities of faith. If the church is to survive the post-modern world in which we find ourselves, we need to individually and collectively, move through fear into safety, through history and tradition into innovation, and through worry into excitement for the future. Thresher's work provides us with a methodology for making these shifts."

—Rev, Dr. Bonnie Bates, Associations Associate Minister for
Congregational Vitality and Development,
Eastern Ohio and Western Reserve Associations of
the Ohio Conference of the United Church of Christ.

Since publication of *The Coming Interspiritual Age* I have constantly emphasized today's challenge is linking vital skill sets with the emerging new global Consciousness. Tom Thresher's new book does exactly that as he expands upon the Immunity to Change vision and techniques of Robert Kegan and his associates. Thresher's masterful interweaving of this message with a detailed understanding of the global transitions re-forming both religion and science worldwide, make this a vital and inspiring book.

— Kurt Johnson PhD, co-author *The Coming Interspiritual Age*.

In his insightful book, Crazy Wisdom: Tools for Evolving Consciousness, Reverend Tom Thresher presents a compelling vision for personal and social transformation. By combining the enduring power of the great wisdom traditions with leading edge psychology and philosophy, Thresher provides an inspiring yet practical approach to spiritual development. It is good to see the new truths of the integral perspective being applied to the challenges of our age.

— Steve McIntosh, author of Evolution's Purpose and Integral Consciousness, and President of The Institute for Cultural Evolution

www.ingramcontent.com/pod-product-compliance
Lightning Source LLC
Chambersburg PA
CBHW072240270326
41930CB00010B/2203